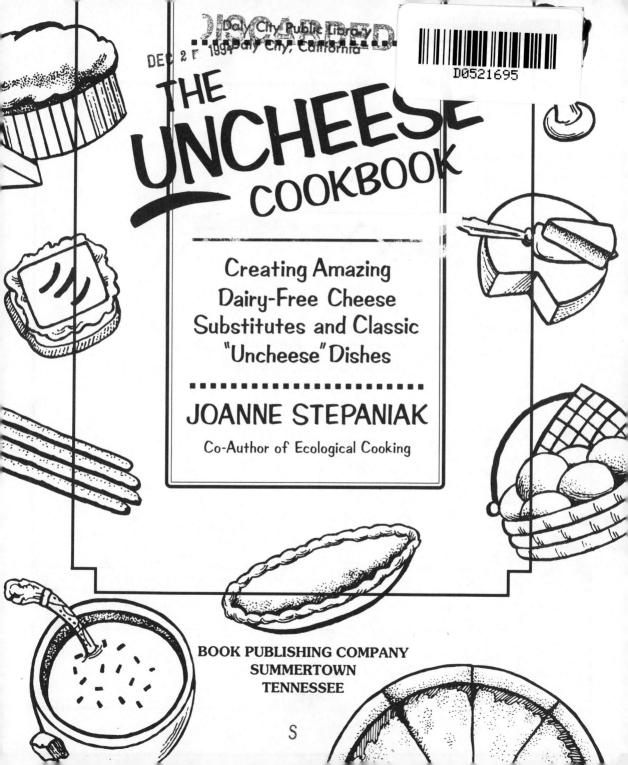

THE UNCHEESE COOKBOOK

Creating Amazing Dairy-Free Cheese Substitutes and Classic "Uncheese" Dishes

· · · · · · · · · · · · · · · · · · · ·

JOANNE STEPANIAK

Co-Author of Ecological Cooking

BOOK PUBLISHING COMPANY
SUMMERTOWN
TENNESSEE

S

641.563
STE

ISBN 0-913990-42-6

Cover design by Nava Atlas
Interior design by Barbara McNew

Special thanks to Doug Farrell for planting a seed that grew.

The Book Publishing Company

P.O. Box 99

Summertown, TN 38483

Stepaniak, Joanne, 1954-
    The uncheese cookbook / by Joanne Stepaniak
        p.   cm.
    Includes bibliographical references (p. 14) and index.
    ISBN 0-913990-42-6
    1. Milk-free diet. 2. Cheese. I. Title.
RM234.5.S74 1994
641.5'63--dc20   93-42489
                                     CIP

Calculations for the nutritional analyses in this book are based on the average number of servings listed with the recipes and the average amount of an ingredient if a range is called for. Calculations are rounded up to the nearest gram. If two options for an ingredient are listed, the first one is used. Not included are optional ingredients, serving suggestions, or fat used for frying, unless the amount of fat is specified in the recipe.

For information on how to arrange an appearance by the author for your group or organization, please write to Joanne Stepaniak, c/o The Book Publishing Company, P.O. Box 99, Summertown, TN 38483.

This book is dedicated to people everywhere who, due to choice or chance, have eliminated cheese from their diet. It is my sincere hope that you will find these recipes gratifying and delicious, and that they satisfy any compelling cheese fantasies you may have.

Enjoy!

Contents

Why an Uncheese Cookbook?

Affluent cultures around the world have had a love affair with cheese for as long as animals have been held in captivity and bred for their resources. Due to its magnificent flavor, amazing adaptability, and insidious way of appeasing our cravings for salt and fat, cheese has been elevated to a position of high nobility. America's infatuation with cheese has spawned some fascinating culinary creations ranging from the classic American cheeseburger to macaroni and cheese and our own beloved version of pizza. Cheese has asserted its influence in every menu category from soups to breads to main courses to even desserts. It is more than a mere condiment or recipe constituent—cheese is an American tradition.

But despite the passion our culture has for its culinary idiosyncrasies, we have been forced to confront the serious repercussions of these dietary habits. Milk and the products made from it are high in fat, cholesterol, and protein, and are completely devoid of dietary fiber. They have been implicated as a causal or exacerbating factor in a myriad of ailments: gastrointestinal disorders including chronic diarrhea, headaches, coronary disease, allergies, respiratory problems, some cancers, iron-deficiency anemia, rheumatoid arthritis, osteoporosis, and obesity. And, despite the fact that most people in other countries around the globe don't drink milk after being weaned and rarely suffer from these medical conditions, the dairy industry continues to bombard us with advertisements professing milk as a "health food" and a necessity to meet calcium requirements.

When we look at other mammals in their natural environment, we discover several similarities among them and glaring differences between them and human beings. All other species of mammals consume their mothers' milk as infants and are eventually weaned, usually after they have tripled their birth weight. Their mothers' milk is nutritionally balanced in fat, protein, and other nutrients for the proper development of that particular species' young. Human beings, it appears, are the only species of mammal that is *never* weaned! No other mammals known continue to drink milk after the weaning stage and certainly never through adulthood. But even more peculiar is that no mammals in their natural environment other than human beings take the milk of *other* species of mammals. The absurdity of this behavior perhaps can best be understood if we envision a pig suckling a cat, or a horse suckling a dog, or—and this is essentially what occurs when we drink milk—a cow suckling a human being. Imagining this brings to light how truly strange and unnatural the consumption of another animal's milk is for the human species. In addition, the ailments mentioned above are rare among other mammals when those animals exist in their natural habitat and consume indigenous foods.

There is a growing number of people worldwide who believe that not only is drinking another species' milk aberrant, but that the utilization of animal foods of any kind inherently and inevitably leads to abuses of human health, the environment, and animals themselves.

Abuses of human health are due to the ingestion of foods that are high in fat, cholesterol, and protein, void of dietary fiber, difficult to digest, and which contain significant quantities of bacteria, chemicals, hormones, and antibiotics. The protein *casein*, found in dairy products, is the leading allergen in the United States. We also have a high incidence of *lactose intolerance*, the inability to digest *lactose*, the sugar in milk. It has been estimated that 18% of American Caucasians are lactose intolerant. Among particular ethnic groups, lactose intolerance is significantly higher. For instance, it has been estimated that 50% of Indians, 58% of Israeli Jews, 65% of Mexican-Americans, 70% of African-Americans, 78% of Arabs and Ashkenazic Jews, and 90% of Asians and North American Indians are lactose intolerant.[1] (Interestingly, the incidence of osteoporosis in Asian and African countries is particularly rare, even though milk is not consumed due to unavailability or lactose intolerance.)

Lactase is the enzyme that breaks down the lactose in milk and milk products and makes them digestible. In human beings, lactase first appears in the intestinal tract of infants during the last trimester of pregnancy, and peaks shortly after birth. Lactase helps us digest human milk, which contains about 75 grams of lactose per quart. Between the ages of one and a half and four years, most children gradually lose lactase activity in their small intestine. This appears to be a normal growth process, one which also occurs in most other mammals shortly after they are weaned. Even though we lose our ability to digest lactose as we mature, when we consume cow's milk we are ingesting about 45 grams of lactose per quart! With aged cheese, much of the lactose is converted to simple sugars during the ripening process— only two percent of the calories are from lactose. For some individuals, this makes cheese much more tolerable than milk. For others, cheese—especially soft, semi-soft, and unripened cheeses (i.e. cottage cheese, ricotta, cream cheese, etc.)—can cause severe gastrointestinal upset.

Then there are abuses which go beyond the personal scope. Environmental damage is caused by a number of processes common in modern society:

---

[1] Robbins, John. *May All Be Fed: Diet for a New World*. New York, NY: William Morrow and Company, Inc., 1992, pp. 109-110

1) the manufacture and use of chemical fertilizers and pesticides used in the production of animal feed,

2) toxins emitted into the atmosphere during transport of animals and animal products,

3) chemical overflow and animal waste products that are disposed into our waterways,

4) the wasteful use of land, water, energy, and other resources used in animal processing.

At a global level, abuses of the earth's terrain include soil erosion and irreparable, environmental depletion of rain forests and other habitats which have been razed to provide crops and grazing land to sustain exorbitant numbers of feed animals.

Then, of course, there are abuses to the animals themselves.

Americans are misled to believe that the milk on their table was supplied by Bessie, a contented cow from Farmer John's idyllic homestead. What we are not told is that Farmer John's homestead is, in reality, a heartless milk factory dedicated to a single purpose—maximum milk production at the cheapest possible cost.

Sweet, gentle Bessie is hardly contented at all. She has been denied the natural life of a cow and the pleasures of foraging, ruminating, and caring for her young. She has been bred, medicated, implanted with hormones, artificially inseminated, and kept perpetually pregnant to provide one thing only—continual production of milk for profit. Her life will be borne out in a cramped, narrow, concrete stall or storage cage for nearly ten months out of the year, chained at the neck and unable to walk or turn around. Three times a day she will be attached to an electric milking machine like just another cog in a factory assembly line. Her natural sensitivity and mellowness will be transformed into so much stress and tension that she must be pacified with tranquilizers. She will be forced to produce three or four times the amount of milk per year as her predecessor a hundred years ago. Her swollen udder will become too large and tender to allow her young to suckle, even if they would be permitted. She will survive a mere four years of this cruel, hollow life, whereas under natural conditions she might live 20 to 25 years. When at last she is unable to keep up the demanded level of milk production, drained and exhausted, Bessie will be packed onto a crowded truck for transport to her final destination—the meat processing plant.

Female calves are born into the same lifelong enslavement as their mothers, but male calves face an even grimmer fate. Shortly after their birth they are sent to auction and purchased by factory farms to live out abbreviated, tormented lives in preparation for their becoming veal. These sweet, big-eyed infants, frisky and playful by nature, are chained, immobile, into crate-like stalls that are 22 inches wide by 54 inches long, barely twice the length and smaller than the width of an unfolded newspaper. They cannot stretch. They cannot turn around. They cannot even turn their head to lick and groom themselves. In fact, they can barely move at all. And as they continue to grow, their stalls seem smaller and smaller around them. Throughout their brief lives, veal calves never experience even the most basic joys of nuzzling and nursing their mother, romping, lying down normally, or even walking! This isolation and confinement causes underdeveloped muscles and keeps the veal flesh light and tender. The calves are also denied their mother's milk, too precious a commodity. In reality, the term "milk-fed veal" is a complete misnomer. The white veal flesh that has become so prized by affluent society is actually a result of deliberate, systematically induced anemia caused by profound iron deprivation. At the age of only four months, if they are able to survive that long, these broken, pitiful, tortured youngsters, who will have endured acts more grisly than most of us can imagine, will be slaughtered for transformation into a gastronomical "delicacy."

There is, sadly, no denying the inextricable correlation between the horrors of meat production and the ghastliness of the dairy industry.

Cheese is the major by-product of these concentration camp-style factories, as it can take up to ten pints of milk to make just one pound of cheese. Because of this, cheese is a concentrated source of fat, cholesterol, hormones, bacteria, and the cumulative antibiotics and other drugs which are routinely ingested by or injected into dairy cows. In addition, aged cheese contains excessive amounts of sodium (about 200 milligrams per ounce) from the salt that is used in processing, along with the molds, enzymes, and yeasts used in various stages of curing. Tyramine, a monoamine found in relatively high amounts in aged cheeses, may trigger the symptoms of migraine headaches.[2] It is also suspected that other amines produced in ripening cheese can interact with nitrates present in the stomach to form nitrosamine, a known carcinogen.[3]

Rennet, an enzyme obtained from the stomach lining of calves, kids, pigs, or lambs, is used to coagulate milk for cheese. Therefore, contrary to prevalent belief, unless ripened cheese is specifically labeled as having been curded with a *vegetable* enzyme, it is *not* a

---

[2]Shils, M. E. and V. R. Young, eds., *Modern Nutrion In Health and Disease*, Seventh Edition. Philadelphia, PA: Lea and Febiger, 1988, p. 1466

[3]Ibid., pp. 1390-1391

vegetarian food! Although soft cheeses and other dairy products such as cottage cheese, ricotta cheese, cream cheese, and sour cream are not ripened, they may also have rennet added to them to make them firmer. Furthermore, they too are exposed to disease-producing organisms, antibiotics, hormones, toxic chemicals, and other harmful substances.

In 1985, forty-seven people in southern California died after eating a Mexican-style soft cheese contaminated with listeria bacteria. This was the largest number of food poisoning deaths recorded in recent United States history.[4] The Center for Science in the Public Interest has recommended that pregnant women and people who are HIV positive, have AIDS, liver disease, cancer, or a weak immune system should avoid soft cheeses such as Mexican-style cheese, Brie, and Camembert.[5]

There are a number of commercial cheese substitutes on the market today. Many of these are made from a soybean base and are high in fat and/or sodium. A majority, especially those which are designed to melt, contain *casein*, the protein in milk. In other words, these "non-dairy" cheeses actually contain a cow's milk derivative, rendering them off limits for those who are allergic to dairy products or wish to avoid them completely. Carefully check the label ingredients of any commercial soy cheese you are considering purchasing or ordering in a restaurant. Casein may also be listed as *caseinate, calcium caseinate,* or *sodium caseinate*. Also check labels for other "hidden" dairy products including whey, milk solids, powdered milk, dried milk cultures, and any other items which sound questionable. A distinct advantage to preparing your own dairy-free "cheezes" over purchasing commercially produced products is that you have control over the fat, sodium, and other ingredients in your food.

As we become more conscious about the abuses in food production in our own country and worldwide, and the effect our dietary choices have on the animals, on our health, and on the environment, there is hope and solace in the knowledge that a dairy-free, totally vegetarian diet is one of the most compassionate, healthful, and empowering life-style changes we can make. And, happily, the transition need not be difficult.

This book was conceived with the awareness that cheese and dairy products are familiar, comfortable, gratifying foods for most Americans, and that changing one's diet is a very

---

[4]Jacobson, Michael F., Ph.D., Lisa Y. Lefferts, and Anne Witte Garland. *Safe Food: Eating Wisely in a Risky World.* New York, NY: The Berkley Publishing Group, 1993, p. 83.

[5]Ibid, p. 10.

personal and emotional decision. It isn't easy to part with foods that conjure up our fondest memories, foods that we've known and loved since childhood and that simply taste just plain good.

Many of the recipes in this book are non-dairy versions of those well-known, heart-warming foods that many of us grew up with and which have become American standards. Others are new creations that will hopefully become classics in your own culinary repertoire. They are not designed to identically duplicate the taste and texture of animal-based cheeses, nor to have a similar nutritional content, but rather to launch our taste buds on exciting new adventures while providing the comfort of familiarity.

All of the recipes are completely dairy-, cholesterol-, and lactose-free, contain no animal products whatsoever, and call only for pure, unadulterated ingredients. Enjoy preparing these wholesome, natural foods—they are easy to make, health-supporting, delicious and cruelty-free. May they bring you abundant joy, well-being, and peace of mind.

For more information about vegan nutrition, contact:

The Vegetarian Resource Group
P.O. Box 1463
Baltimore, MD 21203
(410) 366-VEGE

For more information on dairy production, animal abuse within the dairy industry, and issues related to factory farming, contact:

Farm Sanctuary
P.O. Box 150
Watkins Glen, NY 14891
(607) 583-2225

People for the Ethical Treatment of Animals (PETA)
P.O. Box 42516
Washington, DC 20015
(301) 770-PETA

For more information on the impact of diet on our health and the environment, contact:

EarthSave Foundation
706 Frederick Street
Santa Cruz, CA 95062
(800) 280-1313
(408) 423-4069

About the Nutritional Analyses

Dairy cheese is, by its very nature, high in fat and calories. In *The Uncheese Cookbook*, we have tried to replicate all that is best loved about cheese, while striving to remove or reduce fat wherever feasible and still retain the characteristic "cheesiness" of each recipe. For your convenience, we have provided nutritional breakdowns and suggested serving sizes for the recipes. Current recommended allowances for daily intake of fat range from a liberal 30% of calories from fat (which some health professionals still consider potentially unhealthful), to a conservative but nevertheless achievable 10-20% or less of calories from fat. To determine the percentage of calories from fat in a given food, multiply the number of grams of fat per serving by 9 (calories per gram), divide the answer by the total calories per serving, then multiply by 100. Keep in mind *all* of the foods you will be eating in order to get the complete picture. (For example, if you have *Tofu Creme Cheeze* you will most likely spread it on a low-fat or fat-free bagel and perhaps serve it with vegetables such as carrot sticks or tomato slices. If you prepare a sauce, you would generally serve it over high carbohydrate, low-fat pasta, rice, or potatoes.) Remember to calculate the percentage of calories from fat from the *entire* meal, and use that as a guide when planning your food selections throughout the day to determine your overall intake of fat. Reducing or eliminating the consumption of animal products and oil and keeping high-fat plant foods (i.e. nuts, avocados, coconut, olives, tofu) to a minimum will help to ensure a diet that is within the healthiest recommendations.

At first glance, some of our recipes may appear to be moderately high in fat. Keep in mind that non-dairy cheeze products, like dairy cheeses, should be utilized in much the same way that condiments are—they should add a bit of flavor and substance, but not be the "central attraction." When you round out your fare with fat-free fruits, vegetables, grains, and breads, your overall fat intake will remain within healthful bounds, even with the inclusion of non-dairy, *Uncheese* cheezes. Any fat in our recipes comes solely from natural vegetable sources like nuts or tofu. There are no animal-based fats to add cholesterol to your foods, no hydrogenated or saturated fats, no synthetic fat substitutes or chemical flavor enhancers, and no artificial colors.

If you would like to remove or reduce the fat in any recipe that contains less than one-half cup of nuts or tahini, feel free to halve the amount called for or even eliminate it completely. This will not affect the outcome of the recipe, however it will result in a less rich, less cheesy taste. ***If you use low-fat tofu in place***

of the full-fat variety, you can reduce the fat in recipes calling for tofu to almost nil.

It appears that low-fat cheeses are not immune from the health hazards associated with eating dairy products, and, in some respects, may even be more harmful. John McDougall, M.D., in his book, *The New McDougall Cookbook* (New York: Dutton, 1993, p. 24), states that low-fat dairy products, although an improvement over high-fat varieties, still promote health problems: "When you remove the fat from a milk product, you increase the relative amounts of proteins and lactose. Consuming more protein increases one's likelihood of developing a food allergy and also promotes loss of calcium from the body, leading to osteoporosis. The low-fat varieties still cause lactose-induced bowel problems, as well as additional health problems resulting from fiber, mineral, and vitamin deficiencies." Additionally, when the fat is removed from dairy cheese, the non-fat-soluble toxins in the resulting product are rendered more concentrated.

In addition to fat, salt is the other flavor most often associated with cheese. If any of our recipes seem too highly seasoned with salt or tamari (natural soy sauce) for your tastes, you can successfully reduce the amount called for by up to one-half or, if you prefer, exclude it altogether. In that case, increase the amount of lemon juice or vinegar by one or two tablespoonfuls to balance out the flavors.

A well-rounded, low-fat diet is indeed a valuable objective, and one that *is* attainable. We hope that *The Uncheese Cookbook* will help you to "have your cheese and eat it too."

Resources and Recommended Reading

Barnard, Neal D., M.D. *The Power of Your Plate.* Summertown, TN: The Book Publishing Company, 1990.

Barnard, Neal D., M.D. *Food for Life.* New York, NY: Harmony Books, division of Crown Publishers, Inc., 1993.

Jacobson, Michael F., Ph.D., Lisa Y. Lefferts, and Anne Witte Garland. *Safe Food: Eating Wisely in a Risky World.* New York, NY: The Berkley Publishing Group, 1993.

Klaper, Michael, M.D. *Pregnancy, Children, and the Vegan Diet.* Alachua, FL: Gentle World Publishing, 1987.

Klaper, Michael, M.D. *Vegan Nutrition Pure and Simple.* Alachua, FL: Gentle World Publishing, 1987.

Mason, Jim and Peter Singer. *Animal Factories.* New York, NY: Crown Publishers, 1980.

McDougall, John A., M.D. and Mary A. McDougall. *The McDougall Plan.* Piscataway, NJ: New Century Publishers, Inc., 1983.

McDougall, John A., M.D. *McDougall's Medicine: A Challenging Second Opinion.* Piscataway, NJ: New Century Publishers, Inc., 1985.

McDougall, John A. M.D. and Mary McDougall. *The New McDougall Cookbook.* New York, NY: Dutton, Penguin Books, 1993.

Oski, Frank, M.D. *Don't Drink Your Milk!*, 9th ed. Brushton, NY: TEACH Services, 1992.

Regan, Tom. *The Case for Animal Rights.* Berkeley, CA: University of California Press, 1983.

Rifkin, Jeremy. *Beyond Beef: The Rise and Fall of the Cattle Culture.* New York, NY: Dutton Publishing, 1992.

Robbins, John. *Diet for a New America.* Walpole, NH: Stillpoint Publishing, 1987.

Robbins, John. *May All Be Fed: Diet for a New World.* New York, NY: William Morrow and Company, Inc., 1992.

Singer, Peter. *Animal Liberation*, rev. ed. New York, NY: Avon Books, 1990

Wasserman, Debra and Reed Mangels, Ph.D., R.D. *Simply Vegan.* Baltimore, MD: Vegetarian Resource Group, 1991.

An Important Note

About the Recipe Ingredients

Cheese and the items made from cheese are generally considered to be "fast foods," and this book was created with that concept in mind. Simplicity, speed, and ease of preparation are the watchwords of every recipe.

Wherever possible, we have tried to use ingredients that are common and readily available. However, in order to maintain the highest integrity, wholesomeness, and nutritional values possible, we did find it necessary to incorporate some ingredients that may not be familiar to you. The glossary on page 180 will introduce you to these ingredients and briefly explain their uses and origins. Those items which are not readily available in your local supermarket may be purchased from most natural food stores or from the mail order vendors listed on page 185. Although some ingredients may seem strange at first, know that they are wholesome and natural. Derived only from plant and vegetable sources, these ingredients are much purer and nutritious than their chemical, synthetic, highly refined, or animal counterparts—and much more appetizing. I hope you will enjoy the adventure of exploring these new foods and take advantage of the exciting vistas they hold in store.

About Blending and Processing

Whenever an *Uncheese* recipe calls for using a food processor, be sure to use one that is fitted with a metal blade in order to achieve the best results.

A large number of the recipes in *The Uncheese Cookbook* call for processing different combinations of foods in a blender. This is to effectively replicate the creamy taste and smooth texture of many familiar dairy products. With all of the recipes that call for blending, it is essential to process the foods long enough so that they form a completely smooth sauce or purée. This may require several minutes of blending on low or high speeds and will usually necessitate stopping the blender occasionally to scrape down the sides of the container and stir the contents.

Many *Uncheese* recipes may need to be processed in batches depending on the capacity of your blender container. This is because blender jars vary in size from manufacturer to manufacturer. Please take this into consideration when processing large quantities of food. Don't overfill your blender jar; keep a bit of space available in the top of the container so when the blended mixture temporarily "expands" with air during processing, it can move freely and won't be forced out under the lid rim. It is a wise practice to start with a smaller quantity of food in your blender and add more to it if there is sufficient room.

When puréed in a blender, hot liquids can release a surprising amount of steam which can force the lid to pop off. The heat could even crack the blender jar if it is not heat resistant or thick enough. As a precautionary measure, fill the blender only halfway when processing hot liquids, and use a kitchen towel to hold the lid slightly ajar. To ease the task of cleaning, put a few drops of dish detergent along with a cup of water into the blender jar. Run the blender on low for several seconds prior to washing it.

Purchase the highest quality blender you can afford—one with a powerful motor and thick glass jar that will stand up to hot liquids and heavy loads. A blender with a heavy-duty or commercial motor will work best. A broad range of speeds is not necessary; a high and low switch is sufficient. Personally, we have had the most success with KitchenAid, Waring, and Osterizer blenders. They have rugged, functional containers and strong motors that will produce the smoothest purées. Whichever brand you choose, using sturdy, professional equipment will result in easier, more consistent food processing and years of impeccable service.

A note about vegan cooking

The word *vegan* (VEE-gn) is used in reference to several ingredients throughout this book. It refers to items that do not contain animal products of any kind (the flesh of any animal, fish or bird, eggs, milk, milk products, cheese or honey, for example).

A Comparison of Dairy Cheeses vs. *Uncheezes*

Cheese	Amount	Calories	Fat (gm)	Sodium (mg)	Choles. (mg)	Protein (gm)
American cheese	1 T	35	3	135	9	2.1
process cheese spread	1 T	47	3.4	218	9	2.7
Gee Whiz Spread	*1 T*	*29*	*0*	*39*	*0*	*2*
Swiss cheese	1 oz.	107	7.8	74	26	8.1
Swizz Cheeze	*1 oz.*	*44*	*3*	*65*	*0*	*2*
Muenster cheese	1 oz.	104	8.5	178	27	6.6
Muenster Cheeze	*1 oz.*	*42*	*2*	*137*	*0*	*2*
Colby cheese	1 oz.	112	9.1	171	27	6.7
Colby Cheeze	*1 oz.*	*38*	*1*	*138*	*0*	*1*
cream cheese	1 oz.	99	9.9	84	31	2.1
Tofu Creme Cheeze	*1 oz.*	*25*	*1*	*65*	*0*	*2*
feta cheese	1 oz.	75	6	316	25	4
Betta Feta	*1 oz.*	*34*	*2*	*137*	*0*	*2*
Gruyère	1 oz.	117	9.2	95	31	8.5
Garbanzo Gruyère	*1 oz.*	*35*	*1*	*43*	*0*	*1*
mozzarella (whole)	1 oz.	80	6.1	106	22	5.5
Mostarella	*1 oz.*	*49*	*2*	*141*	*0*	*2*
Parmesan (grated)	1 T	33	1.5	93	4	2.1
Parmazano	*1 T*	*35*	*1*	*51*	*0*	*3*
ricotta (skim)	1/2 cup	171	9.8	155	38	14
Tofu Ricotta	*1/2 cup*	*49*	*3*	*150*	*0*	*4*
Brie	1 oz.	95	7.9	178	28	5.9
Brie Cheeze	*1 oz.*	*52*	*4*	*165*	*0*	*2*

Cheezes, Spreads & Dips

Gee Whiz Spread

Yield: 2 cups

Have you ever longed for good, old-fashioned American cheese? Knowing that it's high in fat, cholesterol, and sodium, you probably took one look and put the packaged slices right back on the shelf. Well, here is an all-American spread you can feel good about. Gee Whiz Spread is an amazing and versatile food which is remarkably fast and simple to prepare. It's great on crackers and sandwiches, or in almost any recipe that calls for dairy cheddar cheese. Spread it on buns and serve with vegetarian burgers for instant "cheezeburgers." Or add a few spoonfuls to your favorite soup or sauce to turn them into cheezy delights.

1 (15.5 oz.) can Great Northern beans (about 1½ C), rinsed well and drained
½ C pimiento pieces, drained
6 T nutritional yeast flakes
3 T fresh lemon juice
2-3 T tahini
½ tsp. onion granules
½ tsp. prepared yellow mustard
½ tsp. salt

Place all the ingredients in a blender, and process until completely smooth. Transfer to a storage container, and chill thoroughly before serving.

Per 2 Tbsp. serving: Calories: 59, Protein: 4 gm., Carbohydrates: 8 gm., Fat: 1 gm.

Colby Cheeze

Yield: one 3-cup brick

A tangy but mild orange cheeze that slices well for sandwiches and snacks. It also makes fantastic grilled cheeze sandwiches and is perfect for grating over salads or baked potatoes.

1½ C water
5 T agar flakes

½ C pimiento pieces, drained
½ C raw cashew pieces
¼ C nutritional yeast flakes
3 T fresh lemon juice
2 T tahini (optional)
2 tsp. onion granules
1 tsp. salt
¼ tsp. garlic granules
⅛ tsp. ground dill seed
⅛ tsp. mustard powder

Place the water and agar flakes in a small saucepan, and bring to a boil. Reduce the heat and simmer for 5 minutes, stirring often. Place in a blender with the remaining ingredients, and process until completely smooth.

Pour immediately into a lightly oiled, 3-cup rectangular mold, loaf pan, or other small, rectangular container, and cool. For round slices, pack into a small, straight-sided, cylindrical container. Cover and chill for several hours or overnight. To serve, turn out of the mold and slice. Store leftovers covered in the refrigerator.

Per 2 Tbsp. serving: Calories: 26, Protein: 1 gm., Carbohydrates: 2 gm., Fat: 1

Olive Cheeze

Prepare *Colby Cheeze*, replacing the ground dill seed and mustard powder with 1 T Dijon mustard. After blending, stir in ¾ C chopped black olives.

Swizz Cheeze

Yield: one 2½-cup brick

A versatile, tangy, white cheeze. Ideal for shredding, melting, toasting in sandwiches, and of course, snacking. Try it on our delicious Reubens, pg. 159, for a truly special treat.

1½ C water
5 T agar flakes

½ C raw cashew pieces
¼ C nutritional yeast flakes
3 T fresh lemon juice
2 T tahini (optional)
1 T onion granules
2 tsp. Dijon mustard
¼ tsp. salt
½ tsp. garlic granules
½ tsp. mustard powder
¼ tsp. ground dill seed

Place the water and agar flakes in a small saucepan, and bring to a boil. Reduce the heat and simmer for 5 minutes, stirring often. Place in a blender with the remaining ingredients, and process until completely smooth.

Pour immediately into a lightly oiled, 3-cup rectangular mold, loaf pan, or other small rectangular container. Cover and chill for several hours or overnight. To serve, turn out of the mold and slice. Store leftovers covered in the refrigerator.

Per 2 Tbsp. serving: Calories: 30, Protein: 1 gm., Carbohydrates: 2 gm., Fat: 1 gm.

Mostarella Cheeze

Yield: 3 cups

This semi-soft cheese may be used just like dairy mozzarella—on pizza, in sandwiches, or as a snack on crackers. Sliceable as well as spreadable.

2 C water
½ C nutritional yeast flakes
⅓ C quick-cooking rolled oats
¼ C tahini
4 T arrowroot or cornstarch
3-4 T fresh lemon juice
1 T onion granules
1 tsp. salt

Process all the ingredients in a blender for several minutes until very smooth.

Pour into a saucepan and cook over medium, stirring constantly, until very thick and smooth.

Pack into a lightly oiled, 3-cup rectangular mold, loaf pan, or other small, rectangular container, and cool. For round slices, pack into a small, straight sided, cylindrical container. Cool, cover, and chill overnight. To serve, turn out of the mold and carefully slice. Store leftovers covered in the refrigerator.

Per 2 Tbsp. serving: Calories: 33, Protein: 2 gm., Carbohydrates: 4 gm., Fat: 1 gm.

Smoky Provolone Cheeze

Prepare *Mostarella Cheeze* as directed but add, to taste, during blending your choice of ½ T hickory-smoked nutritional yeast, ¼-½ tsp. hickory salt, or ¼ tsp. liquid smoke.

Muenster Cheeze

Yield: one 3-cup brick

A mild cheeze that works with almost every food. Serve it in slices with crisp fruits such as pears or apples, add diced cubes to your favorite steamed vegetables, or create cold sandwiches or toasty grilled cheeze.

1½ C water
5 T agar flakes

½ C raw cashew pieces
½ C firm silken tofu, crumbled
¼ C nutritional yeast flakes
¼ C fresh lemon juice
2 T tahini (optional)
1½ tsp. onion granules
1 tsp. salt
½ tsp. mustard powder
¼ tsp. garlic granules
¼ tsp. ground caraway seed

paprika

Place the water and agar flakes in a small saucepan, and bring to a boil. Reduce the heat and simmer for 5 minutes, stirring often. Place in a blender with the remaining ingredients except the paprika, and process until completely smooth. The mixture will be thick.

Lightly oil a 3-cup rectangular mold, loaf pan, or other small rectangular container, and sprinkle paprika over the sides and bottom until lightly coated. Pour in the cheeze and allow to cool. Cover and chill for several hours or overnight. To serve, turn out of the mold and slice. Store leftovers covered in the refrigerator.

Per 2 Tbsp. serving: Calories: 28, Protein: 1 gm., Carbohydrates: 2 gm., Fat: 1 gm.

Monterey Jack Cheeze

Prepare *Muenster Cheeze*, but omit the paprika.

Chunky Roquefort Dip & Dressing

Yield: 2 cups

A rich, chunky, flavorful dressing that is delightful as a dip with raw or steamed vegetables or as a topping for crunchy, fresh salads (particularly ones with beans). Try it with chopped, fresh vegetables over split baked potatoes.

¼ lb. firm regular tofu, coarsely
　　crumbled
1 C water
1 T All-Season Blend, p. 93

1 (10.5 oz.) pkg. firm silken tofu,
　　drained and crumbled
½ C low-fat, dairy-free (vegan) milk
1 T tahini
4 tsp. umeboshi plum paste
1 tsp. nutritional yeast flakes
2 cloves garlic, finely chopped,
　　or 1 tsp. garlic granules
pinch of ground white pepper

1 T fresh parsley, chopped,
　　or 1½ tsp. dried parsley flakes

Place the crumbled firm tofu in a small saucepan with water and All-Season Blend. Bring to a boil. Reduce the heat and simmer for 20 minutes, stirring occasionally. Drain well and set aside.

Place the remaining ingredients except the parsley in a blender, and process until smooth and creamy. The mixture will be very thick. Transfer to a bowl and stir in the crumbled firm tofu and parsley. Cover and chill several hours or preferably overnight before serving.

Per 2 Tbsp. serving: Calories: 30, Protein: 2 gm., Carbohydrates: 1 gm., Fat: 1 gm.

Parmazano

Yield: 1½ cups

Sprinkle this delightful topping over pasta or pizza, use in Uncheese *recipes, or wherever you would normally use Parmesan cheese. It is very easy to make if you have a food processor. If you do not have one, you can grind it in an electric nut, spice, or coffee mill. Blenders are not recommended for grinding almonds, since more time and frequent stopping to stir the mixture are necessary.*

1 C nutritional yeast flakes
½ C raw almonds, blanched and
    patted dry*
½ tsp. salt

Place all the ingredients in a food processor, and process for several minutes until the almonds are very finely ground. Store in a tightly sealed container in the refrigerator.

Per Tbsp. serving: Calories: 35, Protein: 3 gm., Carbohydrates: 3 gm., Fat: 1 gm.

* To blanch almonds, place them in enough water to completely cover. Bring to a boil and simmer for 1-2 minutes. Drain and allow to cool, or rinse under cold tap water for rapid cooling. Pinch skins between thumb and forefinger at the base of each almond. Skins will slip off readily.

Gooda

Yield: one 3-cup dome

A dome-shaped cheeze with a creamy texture and lovely golden color. Slice into wedges for an impressive snack or appetizer.

1¾ C water
½ C carrots, chopped

5 T agar flakes

½ C raw cashew pieces
¼ C nutritional yeast flakes
3 T tahini
3 T fresh lemon juice
1 T Dijon mustard
2 tsp. onion granules
1 tsp. salt
½ tsp. garlic granules
½ tsp. mustard powder
¼ tsp. turmeric
¼ tsp. paprika
¼ tsp. ground cumin

Place the water and carrots in a saucepan, and bring to a boil. Reduce the heat, cover, and cook for 15 minutes. Remove the lid and stir in the agar flakes. Bring to a boil again. Then reduce the heat and simmer for 5 more minutes.

Pour the cooked carrots, water, and agar in a blender and add the remaining ingredients. Process until very smooth.

Pour immediately into a lightly oiled, 3-cup bowl or mold with a rounded bottom. Smooth the top. Cool, cover, and chill several hours or overnight. To serve, turn out of the mold and slice into wedges. Store leftovers covered in the refrigerator.

Per 2 Tbsp. serving: Calories: 37, Protein: 1 gm., Carbohydrates: 3 gm., Fat: 2 gm.

Tofu Cottage Cheeze

Yield: 3½ cups

An excellent replacement for dairy cottage cheese. Try it in scooped out melon halves or with other fresh fruit, as well as with your favorite savory foods. It can also be spooned onto Uncheese blintz wrappers, pg. 152. Gently fold the wrappers over in half for a lovely tofu cottage cheeze stuffed "omelet." Delightful with a dollop of Tofu Sour Cream, pg. 90.

1 lb. firm regular tofu, drained and
    well mashed
⅔ C dairy-free (vegan) mayonnaise
2 tsp. onion granules
1 tsp. garlic granules
1 tsp. salt
1 tsp. ground dill seed
    or ground caraway seed

Place all the ingredients in a bowl, and mix thoroughly. Store in the refrigerator.

Per ½ cup serving: Calories: 107, Protein: 5 gm.,
Carbohydrates: 3 gm., Fat: 7 gm.

Tofu Ricotta

Yield: 5½ cups

Use this non-dairy ricotta in any savory dish that calls for ricotta cheese.

1½ lb. firm regular tofu, well
    mashed
¼ C fresh lemon juice
2 tsp. dried basil leaves
½-1½ tsp. sweetener of your choice
¾ tsp. salt
½ tsp. garlic granules

Mash all the ingredients together until the mixture has a fine, grainy texture like ricotta cheese. Store in the refrigerator.

Per ½ cup serving: Calories: 49, Protein: 4 gm.,
Carbohydrates: 2 gm., Fat: 3 gm.

Betta Feta

Yield: 2 cups (drained)

*This delicious "faux feta" tastes very much like dairy feta and is just as adaptable.
Crumble it over pasta, grains, or raw vegetable salads.*

1 lb. firm regular tofu, drained and
    cut into ¼- or ½-inch cubes
2 C water
2 T All-Season Blend, p. 93

¼ C red wine vinegar
¼ C water
2 T tahini
2 T fresh lemon juice
1 tsp. salt
1 tsp. dried basil leaves
1 tsp. dried oregano leaves
½ tsp. garlic granules

Place the tofu cubes, the 2 cups of water, and the All-Season Blend in a saucepan. Bring to a boil, reduce the heat to medium, and simmer uncovered for 20 minutes, stirring occasionally. Drain and place into a bowl.

In a separate bowl, whisk together the remaining ingredients until well blended. Pour over the tofu and toss carefully. Cover and chill several hours, stirring occasionally to make sure the tofu cubes are evenly coated. Store in the refrigerator; it will keep for a week or more.

Per ¼ cup serving: Calories: 75, Protein: 5 gm., Carbohydrates: 3 gm., Fat: 4 gm.

Garbanzo Havarti

Yield: 2 cups

High in fiber as well as flavor, this zippy cheeze spread is great for sandwiches and snacks. If you use canned beans, it is a snap to prepare.

1 C water
1½ C cooked garbanzo beans, drained
½ C raw cashew pieces
⅓ C nutritional yeast flakes
2 tsp. onion granules
1 tsp. salt
½ tsp. garlic granules
½ tsp. ground dill seed
½ tsp. whole celery seed
¼ C fresh lemon juice

Place all the ingredients in a blender, and process until smooth.

Pour into a saucepan and cook over medium, stirring almost constantly, until very thick (about 15-20 minutes).

Remove from the heat and pack into a 2-cup mold or other small container. Cool, cover, and chill for several hours or overnight.

Per 2 Tbsp. serving: Calories: 61, Protein: 3 gm., Carbohydrates: 7 gm., Fat: 2 gm.

Garbanzo Gruyère

Yield: one 2½-cup brick

A savory, sliceable loaf. Perfect for sandwiches and crackers, this cheeze is at its best when sliced very thinly. Try it as a sandwich filling garnished with egg-free (vegan) mayonnaise, mustard, lettuce, and perhaps a few tomato or cucumber slices.

1¼ C water
¼ C agar flakes

1 C cooked garbanzo beans, drained
2 T tahini
1½ T umeboshi plum paste
2 tsp. onion granules
½ tsp. garlic granules
¼ tsp. mustard powder
⅛ tsp. ground dill seed

Place the water and agar flakes in a small saucepan, and bring to a boil. Reduce the heat and simmer for 5 minutes, stirring often.

Place in a blender with the remaining ingredients, and process until completely smooth. The mixture will be thick.

Pour immediately into a lightly oiled, 3-cup rectangular mold, loaf pan, or other small, rectangular container, and cool. Cover and chill for several hours or overnight. To serve, turn out of the mold and slice. Store leftovers covered in the refrigerator.

Per 2 Tbsp. serving: Calories: 24, Protein: 1 gm., Carbohydrates: 3 gm., Fat: 1 gm.

Brie

Yield: 1 wheel (about 2½ cups)

A lovely round of creamy cheeze. Delectable by itself, on crackers or sandwiches, but especially elegant as a snack or dessert with fresh, crisp apples or pears. This versatile cheeze is also a terrific pizza topping. Slice it thinly or thickly into wedges.

1½ C water
3 T agar flakes

½ C raw cashew pieces
½ C firm silken tofu, crumbled
¼ C nutritional yeast flakes
¼ C fresh lemon juice
2 T tahini (optional)
1½ tsp. onion granules
1 tsp. salt
¼ tsp. garlic granules
⅛ tsp. ground dill seed

1-2 T wheat germ

Place the water and agar flakes in a small saucepan, and bring to a boil. Reduce the heat and simmer for 5 minutes, stirring often.

Place the agar mixture in a blender with the remaining ingredients, except the wheat germ, and process until completely smooth.

Pour immediately into a 2½-cup round, shallow mold or pie plate that has been lightly oiled and dusted with the wheat germ. Cool, cover, and chill several hours or overnight. To serve, turn out by inverting the mold onto a large round plate (the wheat germ side will now be on top), and slice in wedges.

Per 2 Tbsp. serving: Calories: 34, Protein: 2 gm., Carbohydrates: 3 gm., Fat: 1 gm.

Liptauer Käse

Yield: 1¼ cups

This non-dairy version of the classic Hungarian cheese appetizer is both savory and distinctive. Serve it as a dip for vegetables or as a spread for sandwiches or crackers.

1 C firm regular tofu, drained and
    well mashed
⅓ C egg-free (vegan) mayonnaise
1 T capers, rinsed and drained
1 T chives or scallions, minced
2 tsp. umeboshi plum paste
2 tsp. ground caraway seed
1 tsp. mustard powder

paprika (for garnish)

Place the mashed tofu and remaining ingredients, except the paprika, in a food processor, and process into a smooth paste.

To serve, form the mixture into a mound, sprinkle with an ample amount of paprika, and garnish with watercress or salad greens. Or use as a spread for bread, and sprinkle the top of the spread generously with paprika.

If time permits, allow the mixture to rest at room temperature for about 15 minutes to let the flavors blend, or chill for several hours before serving.

Per 2 Tbsp. serving: Calories: 40, Protein: 2 gm., Carbohydrates: 2 gm., Fat: 2 gm.

Boursin Cheeze

Yield: 1¼ cups

A French-inspired garlic, black pepper, and herb cheese that is marvelous on bread but equally delicious on potatoes. Use as a condiment scooped on top of pasta and your favorite tomato-based sauce. It's an elegant appetizer as well; spread it on mildly-flavored whole grain crackers.

1 C firm regular tofu, drained and mashed well
¼ C egg-free (vegan) mayonnaise
1 T umeboshi plum paste
2-3 medium cloves garlic, minced
1 tsp. dried basil leaves
1 tsp. dried marjoram leaves
½ tsp. dried thyme leaves
¼ tsp. freshly ground black pepper
⅛ tsp. ground rosemary

Place the mashed tofu and other ingredients in a food processor, and process into a smooth paste. Chill in a covered container in the refrigerator for several hours or overnight to allow the flavors to blend. Serve cold or at room temperature.

Per 2 Tbsp. serving: Calories: 36, Protein: 2 gm., Carbohydrates: 2 gm., Fat: 2 gm.

Light Tofu Creme Cheeze

Yield: 1 cup

A creamy spread that whips up in minutes, ready to adorn your morning bagels. And for a unique taste delight, try some of the delicious variations listed after the Kefir Cheeze *recipe, pg 36.*

¼ lb. firm regular tofu, patted dry and crumbled
⅓ C firm silken tofu, patted dry and crumbled
1½ T fresh lemon juice
1½ tsp. tamari
½ tsp. nutritional yeast flakes

Place all the ingredients in a food processor, and process until completely smooth. Store in the refrigerator.

Per 2 Tbsp: Calories: 23, Protein: 2 gm., Carbohydrates: 1 gm., Fat: 1 gm.

Rich Tofu Creme Cheeze

Yield: 1¼ cups

Cashews contribute their sweet, buttery taste, a flavor often associated with dairy cream cheese, while tofu provides substance to this rich, tempting spread. For scrumptious vegetarian "lox and cream cheese," top with strips of roasted red peppers.

¼ C raw cashew pieces
3 T water
2 T fresh lemon juice
1 T brown rice syrup,
    or 2 tsp. pure maple syrup
1 C firm regular tofu, patted dry and
    crumbled
¾ tsp. salt
scant pinch of garlic granules

Place the cashew pieces, water, lemon juice, and rice syrup or maple syrup in a blender, and process several minutes into a thick, smooth cream. Add the salt, crumbled tofu, and garlic granules, and process until very smooth. It is essential to blend the mixture for several minutes in order to pulverize the tofu and achieve a velvety smooth consistency. Chill thoroughly before serving.

Per 2 Tbsp: Calories: 52, Protein: 3 gm., Carbohydrates: 3 gm., Fat: 3 gm.

Kefir Cheeze

Yield: 1½ cups

Traditional kefir cheese is a thick, cultured, milk-based product that is a cross between yogurt and cream cheese, and can be used like either one. Our non-dairy version calls for just a few simple ingredients to create kefir's characteristic, sweet-tart flavor. Although it is much lower in fat than cream cheese, it retains the same adaptability as its dairy cousin. Use Kefir Cheeze in any recipe that calls for buttermilk, yogurt, sour cream, or cream cheese. Create instant, fruit-flavored "yogurt" by stirring in a few spoonfuls of naturally sweetened fruit conserves. Kefir also makes a great topping for fresh fruit or vegetables. Try some of the variations which follow.

1 (10.5 oz.) pkg. firm silken tofu, crumbled
1½ T fresh lemon juice
1 T umeboshi plum vinegar
1 T mirin

Process all the ingredients in a food processor or blender until smooth. Chill before serving.

Per 2 Tbsp. serving: Calories: 20, Protein: 2 gm., Carbohydrates: 1 gm., Fat: 1 gm.

Herb Cheeze
Stir in 1 clove minced garlic, and ¼ tsp. each of dried dill weed, crushed rosemary, dried thyme, and parsley flakes.

Caraway Cheeze
Stir in 1 finely minced clove garlic, 1 T chopped capers, and 2 tsp. ground caraway seed.

Date and Nut Spread
Stir in ¼ C chopped walnuts and ¼ C chopped pitted dates.

Pineapple Spread
Stir in ¼ C drained, canned, unsweetened pineapple tidbits.

Vegetable Cheeze
Stir in 1 minced scallion, 1 finely minced clove garlic, 1 small grated carrot, ¼ C minced red or green bell pepper, and ¼ C minced fresh parsley.

Port Wine Uncheese

Yield: 1½ cups

A light purple spread with a rich, distinctive wine and cheddar flavor.

1 (15.5 oz.) can pinto beans (about
 1½ C), rinsed well and drained
¼ C non-alcoholic red wine
2 T sweet white miso
3 T tahini

Blend all the ingredients until very smooth. Chill thoroughly before serving.

Per 2 Tbsp. serving: Calories: 58, Protein: 2 gm., Carbohydrates: 8 gm., Fat: 2 gm.

Herb & Tomato Cheeze Spread

Yield: 1½ cups

A thick, savory, orange spread for bread, crackers, or as a vegetable dip.

1 C water
⅓ C quick-cooking rolled oats
⅓ C fresh lemon juice
¼ C nutritional yeast flakes
3 T unsalted tomato paste
2 T tahini
1 tsp. salt
1 tsp. onion granules
½ tsp. garlic granules
¼ tsp. dried thyme leaves
¼ tsp. paprika
⅛ tsp. ground dill seed
pinch of cayenne pepper (optional)

Place all the ingredients in a blender, and process until the oats are finely ground and the mixture is completely smooth. Pour into a saucepan and cook over medium-high, until very thick, stirring constantly. Chill thoroughly before serving.

Per 2 Tbsp. serving: Calories: 37, Protein: 2 gm., Carbohydrates: 4 gm., Fat: 1 gm.

Garbanatto

Yield: 2 cups

A thick, rich dip without any added fat! Piquant and highly flavored. So luscious it can even be used in place of mayonnaise.

1 (10.5 oz.) pkg. firm silken tofu, drained and crumbled
½ C cooked garbanzo beans, drained
3 T fresh lemon juice
2-3 T onion, chopped
2 T capers, rinsed and drained
1 T red wine vinegar
1 T Vegetarian Worcestershire Sauce, p. 93
2 tsp. Dijon mustard
1 tsp. salt
⅛ tsp. freshly ground black pepper, or to taste
water, as needed

Process all the ingredients in a blender or food processor until very smooth. Add the water, 1 teaspoon at a time, only if necessary to facilitate processing. The consistency should be very thick.

Per 2 Tbsp. serving: Calories: 25, Protein: 2 gm., Carbohydrates: 2 gm., Fat: 1 gm.

Onion, Dill & Horseradish Cheeze

Yield: one 3-cup brick

This piquant cheeze is fragrant and delectable, and easily slices into thick slabs or paper-thin shavings.

1½ C water
5 T agar flakes

½ C raw cashew pieces
¼ C nutritional yeast flakes
3 T fresh lemon juice
2 T tahini
2 T prepared white horseradish (not creamed)
2 tsp. Dijon mustard
1 tsp. salt
1 tsp. onion granules
¼ tsp. garlic granules

3 T dried onion flakes
2 tsp. dried dill weed

Place the water and agar flakes in a small saucepan and bring to a boil. Reduce the heat and simmer for 5 minutes, stirring often.

Place in a blender with the remaining ingredients, except onion flakes and dill weed, and process until completely smooth. By hand, stir in the onion flakes and dill weed.

Pour immediately into a lightly oiled, 3-cup rectangular mold, loaf pan, or other small rectangular container. Cover and chill for several hours or overnight. To serve, turn out of mold and slice. Store leftovers in the refrigerator.

Per 2 Tbsp. serving: Calories: 32, Protein: 1 gm., Carbohydrates: 2 gm., Fat: 1 gm.

Hot Parmesan Artichoke Dip

Yield: 4 cups

A delicious, hot appetizer for vegetable sticks, pita wedges, or chips. Also wonderful on sourdough or Italian bread. Try spreading it on toasted, whole grain bread slices or English muffins, then broil for a few minutes until lightly browned and crusty.

2 (14 oz.) cans artichoke hearts (water-packed), rinsed, drained well, squeezed dry, and quartered

1 (10.5 oz.) pkg. firm silken tofu, drained and crumbled

½ C low-fat, non-dairy (vegan) milk

1 tsp. dried basil leaves

1 tsp. dried oregano leaves

1 tsp. dried marjoram leaves

1 tsp. arrowroot or cornstarch

3 cloves garlic, chopped

½ tsp. salt

1 C Parmazano, p. 25

Place all the ingredients, except the Parmazano, in a blender or food processor, and process until very smooth. Pour into a bowl and stir in the Parmazano. Transfer to a large, lightly oiled pie plate, quiche pan, or shallow casserole dish, and bake at 350°F until lightly crusty on top (about 45-60 minutes, depending on the size of the baking dish). Serve hot, straight from the baking dish.

Per 2 Tbsp. serving: Calories: 35, Protein: 2 gm., Carbohydrates: 4 gm., Fat: 1 gm.

Pecan Cheeze

Yield: 1¼ cups

The flavor of toasted pecans is irresistibly tantalizing, and this delectable spread showcases it well.

½ C pecan halves

1 C firm regular tofu, drained and
    well mashed
¼ C celery, minced
3 T sweet white miso
2 T low-fat, dairy-free (vegan) milk

Place the pecan halves on a dry baking sheet. Bake at 350°F in an oven or toaster oven for 12-15 minutes, until lightly toasted. Cool.

Place the mashed tofu, cooled pecans, and remaining ingredients in a food processor, and process into a smooth paste. Chill in a covered container in the refrigerator for several hours or overnight to allow the flavors to blend.

Per 2 Tbsp. serving: Calories: 68, Protein: 3 gm., Carbohydrates: 3 gm., Fat: 4 gm.

Cold Tomato Cheeze Dip

Yield: 2 cups

A robust, thick sauce that holds its own with crackers, pita wedges, and crunchy raw vegetables. Try it with wide strips of green bell pepper, hunks of black or white radishes, or voluptuous cauliflower florets.

1¼ C water
1 (6 oz.) can unsalted tomato paste
¼ C fresh lemon juice
¼ C raw cashews pieces
¼ C tahini
¼ C nutritional yeast flakes
1 T onion granules
1 tsp. salt
½ tsp. garlic granules

Place all the ingredients in a blender, and process several minutes until smooth and creamy. The mixture will be thick. Store in the refrigerator.

Per 2 Tbsp. serving: Calories: 51, Protein: 2 gm., Carbohydrates: 5 gm., Fat: 2 gm.

Soups & Chowders

Philly Potato Chowder

Yield: 4½ quarts

Hearty chunks of potatoes floating in a rich, cream cheese-flavored broth.

5 C potatoes (about 2 lbs.), peeled and diced
2 large onions, diced
8 C water

1½ C scallions, sliced
2 tsp. garlic granules
2½ tsp. salt

1 C low-fat, dairy-free (vegan) milk
¾ C raw cashew pieces
⅓ C unbleached all-purpose flour
3 T fresh lemon juice
3 T nutritional yeast flakes
2 tsp. onion granules

1 T vegetarian bacon bits

Place the potatoes, onions, and water in a large soup kettle, and bring to a boil. Lower the heat, cover, and simmer for 30 minutes or until the potatoes are fork tender and begin to break down.

Stir in the scallions, garlic powder, and salt. Turn off the heat.

Remove 2 cups of the soup broth with some of the vegetables in it, and place in a blender with the remaining ingredients. Process until completely smooth.

Return the blended ingredients to the soup pot. Cook over medium heat until thickened, stirring constantly. Stir in the vegetarian bacon bits. Warm thoroughly on low without boiling.

Per 1 cup serving: Calories: 100, Protein: 3 gm., Carbohydrates: 16 gm., Fat: 4 gm.

Potato, Tomato & Cheeze Chowder

Yield: 3½ quarts

A thick and satisfying chowder.

2 C potatoes (thin-skinned or
    peeled), diced
1 large onion, chopped
½ C celery, diced
6 C water

2 C low-fat dairy-free (vegan) milk
½ C whole wheat or unbleached
    all-purpose flour
½ C tahini
½ C nutritional yeast flakes
½ C pimiento pieces, drained
2 T fresh lemon juice
2 tsp. onion granules
2 tsp. salt
2 cloves garlic, chopped
½ tsp. mustard powder

¼ C fresh parsley, minced,
    or 4 tsp. dried parsley flakes
1 (16 oz.) can unsalted tomatoes,
    chopped, with juice

Place the potatoes, onion, celery, and water in a large soup kettle, and bring to a boil. Lower the heat, cover, and simmer for 15 minutes, or until the vegetables are tender. To make a *Cheezy Soup Stock,* process the remaining ingredients except the parsley and tomatoes in a blender until completely smooth. Pour the blended ingredients into the soup pot, and cook over medium heat, stirring constantly, until smooth and thickened (about 15-20 minutes). Stir in the parsley and tomatoes. Heat thoroughly but do not boil. Serve hot.

Per 1 cup serving: Calories: 144, Protein: 5 gm., Carbohydrates: 21 gm., Fat: 4 gm.

Vegetables 'N Longhorn Chowder

Yield: 4½ quarts

A substantial and nourishing blend of vegetables, cheeze, and spicy Southwestern flavor.

2 C diced potatoes (thin skinned or
    peeled)
1 large onion, chopped
2 stalks celery, chopped
1 medium carrot, diced
1 red bell pepper, diced
1 green bell pepper, diced
6 C water

Cheezy Soup Stock from Potato,
    Tomato, & Cheeze Chowder,
    p. 46 (use 2 tsp. mustard
    powder, and add ½ tsp.
    Tabasco sauce and ¼ tsp.
    ground white pepper)

½ tsp. dried marjoram leaves
2 C fresh corn,
    or defrosted frozen corn
1 (4 oz.) can chilies, drained and
    chopped
freshly ground black pepper,
    to taste

Place the potatoes, onion, celery, carrot, peppers, and water in a large soup kettle, and bring to a boil. Lower the heat, cover, and simmer for 15 minutes, or until the vegetables are tender. Turn off the heat.

Make the *Cheezy Soup Stock* as on pg. 46, adjusting the ingredients as noted. Pour the blended ingredients into the soup pot along with the marjoram, corn, chilies, and black pepper. Cook over medium-low, stirring almost constantly, until smooth and slightly thickened, about 15-20 minutes. Do not boil. Serve hot.

Per 1 cup serving: Calories: 97, Protein: 4 gm., Carbohydrates: 12 gm., Fat: 3 gm.

Zucchini Chedda Soup

Yield: 3½ quarts

A rich, tempting broth with lots of delicate zucchini. Cheese lovers will adore it!

6 medium zucchini, diced
1 large onion, diced
8 C water

1 C pimiento pieces, drained
½ C tahini
½ C quick-cooking rolled oats
⅓ C nutritional yeast flakes
½ C raw cashew pieces
4 T tamari
3 T fresh lemon juice
1 T dried oregano leaves
2 tsp. salt
3 cloves garlic, chopped
¼ tsp. ground dill seed
¼ tsp. ground allspice
freshly ground black pepper,
    to taste

Place the zucchini, onion, and water in a large soup kettle, and bring it to a boil. Lower the heat and simmer for 20-25 minutes, or until the vegetables are very tender.

Place 2 cups of the soup broth, including some of the cooked onion and zucchini, in a blender with the remaining ingredients. Process until very smooth.

Return the blended ingredients to the soup pot. Heat gently, stirring often, until slightly thickened and warmed through, about 10 minutes. Do not boil.

Per 1 cup serving: Calories: 128, Protein: 5 gm., Carbohydrates: 12 gm., Fat: 6 gm.

Zucchini, Chedda, and Rice Soup
Add 1 C of cooked rice to *Zucchini Chedda Soup* while it is warming through.

Vegetable Scamorze Soup

Yield: 3 quarts

Even people who don't appreciate the wonders of broccoli or cauliflower will find this delicately cheeze-flavored soup irresistible. Its sumptuous, soothing base is hearty, lightly cheesy, and chock full of gorgeous vegetables.

4 C cauliflower and/or broccoli
   florets
1 large onion, chopped
1 C celery, diced
6 C water

2 C low-fat, dairy-free (vegan) milk
½ C whole wheat or unbleached
   all-purpose flour
½ C pimiento pieces, drained
½ C raw cashew pieces
½ C nutritional yeast flakes
¼ C fresh lemon juice
2 T tahini
1 T tamari
1 T onion granules
2 tsp. salt
1 tsp. mustard powder
½ tsp. turmeric

Place the cauliflower, onion, celery, and water in a large soup kettle, and bring to a boil. Lower the heat, cover, and simmer for about 10-15 minutes, or until the vegetables are tender.

Place 2 cups of the soup broth, including some of the cooked vegetables, in a blender with the remaining ingredients. Process until very smooth.

Pour the blended ingredients into the soup pot, and cook over medium, but do not boil. Stir almost constantly until smooth and slightly thickened (about 15-20 minutes). Serve hot.

Per 1 cup serving: Calories: 117, Protein: 6 gm., Carbohydrates: 13 gm., Fat: 4 gm.

Farmhouse Chedda & Yam Soup

Yield: 2 quarts (serves 6)

Golden vegetables and a delicate cheese flavor blend intriguingly in this appealing soup. Use leftover cooked yams if you have them on hand. Otherwise, bake fresh ones in a 400°F oven until soft when squeezed (about 1 hour). Then cool, peel, and mash. Garnish the soup with bite-size croutons or toasted sunflower or pumpkin seeds.

2 C water
2 medium carrots, sliced
1 medium onion, chopped
1 green bell pepper, chopped
2 T All-Season Blend, p. 93
½ tsp. ground cinnamon

2 C cooked yams, mashed
½ C nutritional yeast flakes

2 C low-fat, dairy-free (vegan) milk
2 T Vegetarian Worcestershire
      Sauce, p. 93
salt and freshly ground black
      pepper, to taste

Place the first six ingredients in a large soup pot, and bring to a boil. Reduce the heat to medium, cover, and simmer until the carrots are very tender, about 20 minutes. Turn off the heat and stir in the mashed yams and nutritional yeast.

Pureé the mixture in a blender, a portion at a time, until smooth. Return to the soup pot, and stir in the milk, Worcestershire Sauce, salt, and pepper. Warm over medium heat, until heated through, stirring often.

If the soup is too thick for your liking, thin it gradually with a small amount of low-fat dairy-free (vegan) milk until you achieve the desired consistency.

Per 1⅓ cup serving: Calories: 143, Protein: 7 gm., Carbohydrates: 27 gm., Fat: 1 gm.

Orange, Edam, and Brussels Sprouts Soup

This is a scrumptious soup—lovely green Brussels sprouts bobbing in a rich, colorful sea, seasoned with just a touch of orange, cinnamon, and caraway.

Prepare *Farmhouse Chedda and Yam Soup,* adding 2 tsp. ground caraway seed along with the cinnamon. Omit the Worcestershire Sauce, and replace 1 C of the milk with 1 C of orange juice.

Steam 1 lb. fresh Brussels sprouts, quartered, or 1 lb. frozen Brussels sprouts, until tender, about 10 minutes. (If you use very tiny Brussels sprouts, they may be kept whole.) Stir the cooked Brussels sprouts into the soup, and warm over medium heat, until heated through, stirring often.

Per 1 ⅓ cup serving: Calories: 173, Protein: 7 gm., Carbohydrates: 34 gm., Fat: 1 gm.

Ch-easy Bean & Noodle Soup

Yield: 2½ quarts (serves 6)

Nutritious, soothing, simple, and fast. The perfect broth and noodle soup any time you like.

8 C water
1 (15 oz.) can garbanzo beans,
    rinsed and drained
4 T All-Season Blend, p. 93

1¼ C uncooked small pasta of your
    choice

Place the water, beans, and seasoning in a large soup pot. Stir well and bring to a boil. Add the pasta and simmer until it is cooked al dente. Serve at once.

Per serving: Calories: 165, Protein: 8 gm., Carbohydrates: 28 gm., Fat: 1 gm.

Curried Cauliflower Cheeze Soup

Yield: 3½ quarts

The flavor and aroma of curry and cheeze is absolutely tantalizing—it lifts the spirits and soothes the soul. Perfect any season of the year!

2 medium stalks celery, diced
1 large onion, chopped
1 large head cauliflower, broken into
    bite-size florets
6 C water

2 C low-fat, dairy-free (vegan) milk
½ C tahini
½ C nutritional yeast flakes
½ C unbleached all-purpose flour
2 T tamari
2 T fresh lemon juice
2 T fresh gingerroot, grated,
    or 2 tsp. ground ginger
1 T ground cumin

1 T ground coriander
2 tsp. turmeric
2 tsp. salt
1 tsp. ground cinnamon
3 cloves garlic, chopped
¼ tsp. freshly ground black pepper, or to
    taste
¼ tsp. ground cloves
⅛-¼ tsp. cayenne powder, or to taste
⅛ tsp. ground dill seed

1 C frozen green peas, thawed
3 T fresh dill weed, minced,
    or 1 T dried dill weed

Place the celery, onion, cauliflower, and water in a large soup pot or Dutch oven, and bring to a boil. Reduce the heat, cover, and simmer, stirring occasionally, until the cauliflower is tender (about 10-15 minutes).

Place the remaining ingredients, except the peas and dill weed, in a blender, and process until very smooth. Pour the blended ingredients into the soup pot. Stir in the peas and dill weed. Heat gently until thickened and warmed through (about 10 minutes), but do not boil.

Per 1 cup serving: Calories: 112, Protein: 6 gm., Carbohydrates: 12 gm., Fat: 5 gm.

French Onion Soup Gruyère

Yield: 6 servings

A French classic, known for its gooey topping of luscious cheeses. This one rivals the best of them.

3 large onions, thinly sliced (about
    4-5 C)
½ C water
3 cloves garlic, minced

7½ C water
⅓ C tamari
2 T All-Season Blend, p. 93
¼ tsp. freshly ground black pepper

1 C water
2 T fresh lemon juice
2 T tahini
2 T nutritional yeast flakes
2 T quick-cooking rolled oats
4 tsp. arrowroot or cornstarch
1½ tsp. onion granules
¼ tsp. salt

6 (½-inch thick) slices French bread,
    toasted
¼ C Parmazano, p. 25

To make the onion broth, combine the onions, water, and garlic in a large saucepan or soup kettle. Cover and cook over medium-low heat, stirring occasionally, for 45 minutes, or until the onions are tender. Add more water, if necessary, to keep the onions from sticking. Stir in the next four broth ingredients, and bring to a boil. Reduce the heat, cover and simmer for 15 minutes.

To make the Gruyère Cheeze, place the next eight ingredients in a blender, and process several minutes until the oats are finely ground and the sauce is completely smooth. Pour into a small saucepan and cook over medium, stirring constantly, until smooth and thick (about 5-8 minutes). Cover and set aside.

Place 1 slice of the toasted bread in the bottom of each of six soup bowls. Ladle the soup over the bread. Top each serving with several spoonfuls of the Gruyère Cheeze, and sprinkle with 2 teaspoons of the Parmazano. Serve immediately.

For an interesting variation, ladle the soup into six soup bowls. Spread the toast slices with a thick layer of the Gruyère Cheese. Float the toast, cheeze side up, on top of the soup, and garnish each serving with 2 teaspoons of the Parmazano. Serve immediately.

Per serving: Calories: 230, Protein: 9 gm., Carbohydrates: 35 gm., Fat: 5 gm.

Eggplant Parmagiano Stew

Yield: 4 quarts (8 servings)

An unusual and quick way to serve eggplant! Chunks of eggplant mingle with white beans in a rich, creamy broth. If you prefer an even thicker stew, add a cup or two of cooked pasta or rice before serving.

8 C water
1 (6 oz.) can unsalted tomato paste
1 T garlic granules
1 large onion, chopped
1 medium eggplant, unpeeled and
   chopped
2 C kale, finely chopped,
   or 1 (10 oz.) pkg. frozen chopped
   kale, thawed (optional)
2 (16 oz.) cans Great Northern
   beans, rinsed well and drained
½ C nutritional yeast flakes
2 tsp. dried oregano leaves
¾ tsp. salt, or to taste
freshly ground black pepper
2 fresh, ripe tomatoes, chopped

Combine the water, tomato paste, and garlic granules in a large soup pot. Add the onion, eggplant, and kale, if using. Bring to a boil. Reduce the heat, cover, and simmer over medium heat until eggplant is tender but still firm (about 15 minutes).

Place 2 cups of the soup broth, 1 can of beans, the nutritional yeast, and the seasonings in a blender. Process until very smooth. Pour into the soup pot and mix well. Stir in the remaining can of beans and the chopped, fresh tomatoes. Simmer, uncovered, until the beans are heated through and the tomatoes are slightly softened.

Per 2 cup serving: Calories: 212, Protein: 12 gm., Carbohydrates: 39 gm., Fat: 0 gm.

Fondues & Rarebits

Swiss Fondue

Yield: 3½ cups (serves 6-7)

This thick, cheesy sauce makes a superb fondue dip for crusty, whole grain bread cubes, seitan chunks, and raw or lightly steamed vegetables.

3 C water
½ C nutritional yeast flakes
⅓ C quick-cooking rolled oats
¼ C fresh lemon juice
¼ C tahini
4 T arrowroot or cornstarch
4 tsp. onion granules
1 tsp. salt
½ tsp. mustard powder

Place all the ingredients in a blender, and process several minutes until the oats are finely ground and the sauce is completely smooth. Pour into a saucepan and bring to a boil, stirring constantly. Reduce the heat to low, and continue to cook for a few more minutes, stirring constantly, until thick and smooth. Transfer to a fondue pot, and keep warm over a very low flame.

Per serving: Calories: 131, Protein: 6 gm., Carbohydrates: 15 gm., Fat: 5 gm.

Swiss Raclette

Raclette is a popular Swiss snack or supper favorite made from melted cheese. To make non-dairy Raclette, follow the recipe for *Swiss Fondue*, but spoon the sauce onto individual serving plates so guests can spread it directly on bread or boiled potatoes, pearl onions, and pickles.

Classic Fondue

Yield: 3½ cups (serves 6-7)

Elegant and exotic, with an appealing, sophisticated flavor.

2 C non-alcoholic white wine
1 C water
½ C nutritional yeast flakes
⅓ C quick-cooking rolled oats
¼ C tahini
4 T arrowroot or cornstarch
2 T fresh lemon juice
2 T onion granules
1 tsp. salt
½ tsp. mustard powder
⅛ tsp. ground white pepper
pinch of freshly grated nutmeg,
    or ground nutmeg

Place all the ingredients in a blender, and process several minutes until the oats are finely ground and the sauce is completely smooth. Pour into a saucepan and bring to a boil, stirring constantly. Reduce the heat to low, and continue to cook for a few more minutes, stirring constantly, until thick and smooth. Transfer to a fondue pot, and keep warm over a very low flame.

Per serving: Calories: 154, Protein: 7 gm., Carbohydrates: 20 gm., Fat: 5 gm.

Rosé Fondue

Replace the non-alcoholic white wine with an equal amount of non-alcoholic rosé or red wine.

Chedda Fondue

Yield: 4 cups (serves 8)

Liquid gold—undeniably opulent and luscious. Fabulous with raw mushrooms, cauliflower chunks, and squares of sesame or herbed whole grain bread.

2¾ C water
1 C pimiento pieces, drained
½ C raw cashew pieces
⅓ C quick-cooking rolled oats
⅓ C nutritional yeast flakes
4 T arrowroot or cornstarch
3 T fresh lemon juice
1 T tahini,
    or 2 T sesame seeds
1 T onion granules
1 tsp. salt
2 cloves garlic, chopped
½ tsp. mustard powder
¼ tsp. Tabasco sauce, or more to
    taste
¼ tsp. freshly grated nutmeg,
    or ground nutmeg
¼ tsp. paprika

Place all the ingredients in a blender, and process several minutes until the oats are finely ground and the sauce is completely smooth. Pour into a saucepan and bring to a boil, stirring constantly. Reduce the heat to low, and continue to cook for a few more minutes, stirring constantly, until thick and smooth. Transfer to a fondue pot, and keep warm over a very low flame.

Per serving: Calories: 120, Protein: 4 gm., Carbohydrates: 14 gm., Fat: 5 gm.

Hot Chedda Sauce

This can take the place of melted cheese in most conventional recipes and is a classic over green beans, broccoli, or asparagus.

Prepare *Chedda Fondue*, using ½ C nutritional yeast flakes and ¼ C lemon juice. Reduce rolled oats to ¼ C.

Pub Fondue

Yield: 3½ cups (serves 6-7)

A luxurious, cheddary fondue with the tang and gusto of beer.

2 (12 oz. bottles) non-alcoholic lager
    beer (3 cups)
½ C pimiento pieces, drained
½ C nutritional yeast flakes
⅓ C raw cashew pieces
¼ C quick-cooking rolled oats
4 T arrowroot or cornstarch
1 T onion granules
2 cloves garlic, minced,
    or ½ tsp. garlic granules
1 tsp. mustard powder
¼ tsp. ground white pepper
½ tsp. salt

Place all the ingredients in a blender, and process several minutes until the oats are finely ground and the sauce is completely smooth. Pour into a saucepan and bring to a boil, stirring constantly. Reduce the heat to low, and continue to cook for a few more minutes, stirring constantly, until thick and smooth. Transfer to a fondue pot, and keep warm over a very low flame.

Per serving: Calories: 137, Protein: 6 gm., Carbohydrates: 20 gm., Fat: 4 gm.

Danish Fondue

Yield: 3½ cups (serves 6-7)

Vegetarian bacon bits add enticing flavor and texture. Try this fondue with small sweet gherkins and whole grain rye bread.

2 (12 oz. bottles) non-alcoholic
    beer (3 cups)
½ C nutritional yeast flakes
⅓ C raw cashew pieces
¼ C quick-cooking rolled oats
4 T arrowroot or cornstarch
1½ T onion granules
2 cloves garlic, minced,
    or ½ tsp. garlic granules
½ tsp. mustard powder

2 T vegetarian bacon bits

Place all the ingredients, except the vegetarian bacon bits, in a blender, and process several minutes until the oats are finely ground and the sauce is completely smooth. Pour into a saucepan, add the vegetarian bacon bits, and bring to a boil, stirring constantly. Reduce the heat to low, and continue to cook for a few more minutes, stirring constantly, until thick and smooth. Transfer to a fondue pot, and keep warm over a very low flame.

Per serving: Calories: 137, Protein: 7 gm., Carbohydrates: 18 gm., Fat: 4 gm.

Fruit Fondue

Yield: 3¼ cups (serves 6-7)

Try this delicately flavored, gently sweetened, Swiss-style fondue with fresh seasonal fruits for a light, refreshing brunch or dessert. Apple wedges, naval orange slices, banana wheels, and chunks of whole grain cinnamon raisin bread are particularly inviting.

3 C unsweetened apple juice
   or cider
⅓ C nutritional yeast flakes
⅓ C quick-cooking rolled oats
¼ C raw cashew pieces
4 T arrowroot or cornstarch
2 T tahini
2 T fresh lemon juice
¾ tsp. salt
pinch of freshly grated nutmeg,
   or ground nutmeg
pinch of ground cinnamon

Place all the ingredients in a blender, and process several minutes until the oats are finely ground and the sauce is completely smooth. Pour into a saucepan and bring to a boil, stirring constantly. Reduce the heat to low, and continue to cook for a few more minutes, stirring constantly, until thick and smooth. Transfer to a fondue pot, and keep warm over a very low flame.

Per serving: Calories: 169, Protein: 5 gm., Carbohydrates: 26 gm., Fat: 5 gm.

Caraway Edam Fondue

Yield: 3¾ cups (serves 6-7)

Serve with whole baby mushrooms and cubes of dense pumpernickel bread.

3 C water
¾ C raw carrots, chopped
½ C nutritional yeast flakes
⅓ C quick-cooking rolled oats
¼ C tahini
4 T arrowroot or cornstarch
3 T fresh lemon juice
1½ T onion granules
1 T ground caraway seeds
1 tsp. salt
½ tsp. mustard powder

Place all the ingredients in a blender, and process several minutes until the oats are finely ground, the carrots are pulverized, and the sauce is completely smooth. Pour into a saucepan and bring to a boil, stirring constantly. Reduce the heat to low, and continue to cook for a few more minutes, stirring constantly, until thick and smooth. Transfer to a fondue pot, and keep warm over a very low flame.

Per serving: Calories: 128, Protein: 6 gm., Carbohydrates: 15 gm., Fat: 5 gm.

Onion or Shallot Fondue

Heat ¼ C water and 1 T balsamic vinegar, fresh lemon juice, or non-alcoholic white wine in a large saucepan. Add ½ lb. sweet red onions or shallots, minced, and cook, covered, until tender (about 10 minutes). Continue as for *Caraway Edam Fondue*, omitting the raw carrots and caraway seeds. Add the blended mixture to the onions and cook as above. Stir in ¼ C snipped chives or thinly sliced scallions and freshly ground black pepper, to taste. Serve in a fondue pot.

Smoky Fondue

Yield: 3½ cups (serves 6-7)

A gentle, smoky quality mingles with the delicate onion and beer flavors in this interesting and unusual fondue. Delicious with whole grain bread cubes and thick slices of cooked tofu frankfurters.

2 (12 oz. bottles) non-alcoholic
   beer (3 C)
½ C onion, chopped
⅓ C raw cashew pieces
⅓ C quick-cooking rolled oats
⅓ C nutritional yeast flakes
4 T arrowroot or cornstarch
2 T hickory smoked nutritional yeast
   (Bakon yeast),
    or ½ tsp. liquid smoke
1 T stone ground mustard,
    or Dijon mustard
½ tsp. garlic granules
½ tsp. salt

Place all the ingredients in a blender, and process several minutes until the oats are finely ground and the sauce is completely smooth. Pour into a saucepan and bring to a boil, stirring constantly. Reduce the heat to low, and continue to cook for a few more minutes, stirring constantly, until thick and smooth. Transfer to a fondue pot, and keep warm over a very low flame.

Per serving: Calories: 121, Protein: 4 gm., Carbohydrates: 17 gm., Fat: 4 gm.

Leek Fondue

Yield: 3½ cups (serves 6-7)

Serve with cauliflower florets, steamed potato chunks, radishes, and mushrooms.

½ lb. leeks (about 1 large)
⅓ C water

2 (12 oz. bottles) non-alcoholic
    beer (3 cups)
½ C nutritional yeast flakes
⅓ C quick-cooking rolled oats
4 T tahini
4 T arrowroot or cornstarch
1½ T onion granules
2 cloves garlic, minced,
    or ½ tsp. garlic granules
½ tsp. mustard powder
freshly ground black pepper,
    to taste

Clean the leeks thoroughly, spreading the leaves as you rinse them to remove all of the grit and sand. Mince them finely—a food processor will work best.

Heat the water in a large saucepan, and add the leeks. Cover and cook over medium, stirring often, until tender (about 10-15 minutes).

Place the remaining ingredients in a blender, and process several minutes until the sauce is completely smooth. Pour into the saucepan with the leeks, and bring to a boil, stirring constantly. Reduce the heat to low, and continue to cook until thick and smooth, stirring constantly. Transfer to a fondue pot, and keep warm over a very low flame.

Per serving: Calories: 157, Protein: 6 gm., Carbohydrates: 22 gm., Fat: 5 gm.

Mushroom Fondue

Yield: 3 cups (serves 6)

Serve with florets of lightly steamed broccoli, cubed whole grain bread, quartered red skin potatoes, carrot wedges steamed until tender crisp, and chunks of seasoned seitan.

2 T water + 1 T fresh lemon juice or
 mirin,
 or 3 T non-alcoholic white wine
1 lb. mushrooms, chopped
3 cloves garlic, chopped

2½ C water
⅓ C quick-cooking rolled oats
4 T All-Season Blend, p. 93
4 T tahini
4 T arrowroot or cornstarch
1½ T onion granules
dash of cayenne pepper,
 or several drops Tabasco sauce

Heat the water and lemon juice or wine in a large saucepan, and braise the mushrooms and garlic over medium for 10 minutes.

Place the remaining ingredients in a blender, and process several minutes until smooth. Add the cooked mushrooms and their cooking liquid to the mixture in the blender, and purée. (You may need to process only half of the mixture at a time.)

Return to the saucepan and bring to a boil, stirring constantly. Reduce the heat to low, and cook until thickened and smooth, stirring constantly. Transfer to a fondue pot, and keep warm over a very low flame.

Per serving: Calories: 117, Protein: 3 gm., Carbohydrates: 14 gm., Fat: 4 gm.

Pizza Fondue

Yield: 3¾ cups (serves 6-8)

Lightly steamed baby mushrooms, black olives, cherry tomatoes, sweet red bell pepper squares, cooked pearl onions, pepperoni-flavored seitan, tofu sausages, and French bread cubes are all ideal accompaniments to this spicy "pizza in a pot."

3 C water
½ C nutritional yeast flakes
⅓ C quick-cooking rolled oats
¼ C tahini
4 T arrowroot or cornstarch
4 T fresh lemon juice
4 T unsalted tomato paste
1 T onion granules
1½ tsp. garlic granules
1 tsp. salt

3 T water + 1 T balsamic vinegar,
    fresh lemon juice,
    or non-alcoholic red wine
4 cloves garlic, minced
¼ tsp. crushed red pepper flakes
1½ tsp. dried oregano leaves
½ tsp. dried basil leaves
¼ tsp. dried marjoram leaves
lots of freshly ground black pepper,
    to taste

Place the first ten ingredients in a blender, and process several minutes until the sauce is completely smooth. Set aside.

Heat the water and vinegar (or lemon juice or wine) in a large saucepan, and cook the garlic until barely golden. Add the red pepper flakes, and cook for 20 seconds longer.

Pour the blended mixture into the garlic. Stir in the oregano, basil, marjoram, and pepper, and bring to a boil, stirring constantly. Reduce the heat to low, and continue to cook for a few more minutes, stirring constantly, until thick and smooth. Transfer to a fondue pot, and keep warm over a very low flame.

Per serving: Calories: 94, Protein: 2 gm., Carbohydrates: 12 gm., Fat: 5 gm.

South-of-the-Border Fondue

Yield: 3½ cups (serves 6-7)

A savory fondue, spiced with exotic chili seasonings. Serve it with baby pickled corn, cucumber chunks, sweet red bell pepper squares, radishes, and black olives or avocado pieces lightly sprinkled with lemon juice.

3 C water
½ C nutritional yeast flakes
⅓ C quick-cooking rolled oats
¼ C tahini
4 T fresh lemon juice
4 T arrowroot or cornstarch
2 T onion granules
1 tsp. garlic granules
1 tsp. salt
½ tsp. mustard powder
pinch of ground allspice

¼ C water + 1 T fresh lemon juice, balsamic vinegar or non-alcoholic white wine
4 cloves garlic, minced

2 tsp. paprika
1 tsp. ground cumin
¼ tsp. ground coriander
¼ tsp. turmeric
pinch of cayenne pepper

1 (4 oz.) can peeled and chopped mild green chilies
1 tsp. dried oregano leaves
½ tsp. dried basil leaves
¼ tsp. dried marjoram leaves

Place the first 11 ingredients in a blender, and process several minutes until the sauce is completely smooth. Set aside.

Heat the water and lemon juice, vinegar, or wine in a large saucepan, and cook the garlic for about 2 minutes, just until softened. Stir in the next five spices, and cook for 30 seconds, stirring constantly.

Pour the blended mixture into the garlic. Stir in the chilies and herbs. Proceed as for *Swiss Fondue*, pg. 56.

Per serving: Calories: 130, Protein: 6 gm., Carbohydrates: 16 gm., Fat: 5 gm.

Deviled Fondue

Yield: 3½ cups (serves 6-7)

Zippy and rich—a magnificent dipping sauce. Wonderful with cubes of toasted whole grain bread.

3 C water
½ C nutritional yeast flakes
½ C pimiento pieces, drained
⅓ C quick-cooking rolled oats
¼ C fresh lemon juice
4 T tahini
4 T arrowroot or cornstarch
2 tsp. onion granules
1 tsp. salt (reduce by ¼ tsp. if using hickory salt)
½ tsp. hickory salt, 1 tsp. hickory smoked nutritional yeast, or ½ tsp. liquid smoke, to taste
½ tsp. Tabasco sauce, or more to taste
3 cloves garlic, chopped

1 T prepared yellow mustard
1 T Vegetarian Worcestershire Sauce, p. 93
1 T prepared white horseradish (not creamed)

Place the first 12 ingredients in a blender, and process several minutes until the oats are finely ground and the sauce is completely smooth. Pour into a saucepan and bring to a boil, stirring constantly. Reduce the heat to low, and continue to cook for a few more minutes, stirring constantly, until thick and smooth. Stir in the mustard, Worcestershire Sauce, and horseradish after the fondue has cooked. Transfer to a fondue pot, and keep warm over a very low flame.

Per serving: Calories: 136, Protein: 6 gm., Carbohydrates: 16 gm., Fat: 5 gm.

Curried Cheeze Fondue

Yield: 3½ cups (serves 6-7)

A spicy and tantalizing fondue—especially for curry lovers! Delightful with steamed cauliflower florets, seitan chunks, cubes of lightly steamed zucchini, and whole baby mushrooms.

1½ C water
1½ C non-alcoholic white wine
⅓ C quick-cooking rolled oats
⅓ C nutritional yeast flakes
4 T tahini
4 T arrowroot or cornstarch
2 T onion granules
1 T fresh gingerroot, grated,
    or 1 tsp. ground ginger
1 T ground cumin
1 T ground coriander
1 tsp. salt
1 tsp. turmeric
½ tsp. mustard powder
½ tsp. ground cinnamon
2 cloves garlic, chopped
⅛-¼ tsp. cayenne powder, or to
    taste
⅛-¼ tsp. freshly ground black
    pepper, or to taste
⅛ tsp. ground cloves

2 tsp. dried dill weed (optional)

Place all the ingredients except the dill weed in a blender, and process several minutes until the oats are finely ground and the sauce is completely smooth. Pour into a saucepan, add the dill weed, and bring to a boil, stirring constantly. Reduce the heat to low, and continue to cook for a few more minutes, stirring constantly, until thick and smooth. Transfer to a fondue pot, and keep warm over a very low flame.

Per serving: Calories: 124, Protein: 5 gm., Carbohydrates: 16 gm., Fat: 5 gm.

Buttered Corn Fondue

Yield: 2 cups (serves 2-4)

Corn is naturally sweet and creamy. Its rich, buttery taste bursts forth in this delightfully simple purée. Serve it with broiled or pan-fried tempeh squares, baked yam chunks, lightly steamed broccoli florets, and an artfully adorned green salad on the side. The recipe is easily doubled for larger groups.

1 (16 oz.) pkg. frozen corn, thawed under hot tap water and drained
½ C low-fat, dairy-free (vegan) milk
1 T cornstarch
½ tsp. salt, or to taste
freshly ground black pepper, to taste
several drops Tabasco sauce

Purée all the ingredients in a blender until fairly smooth. Pour into a medium saucepan, and bring to a boil, stirring constantly. Reduce the heat to medium-low, and continue to cook, stirring constantly, until thickened and smooth (about 3-4 minutes). Transfer to a fondue pot, and keep warm over a low flame.

Per serving: Calories: 148, Protein: 3 gm., Carbohydrates: 33 gm., Fat: 0 gm.

Tomato Rarebit

Yield: 2½ cups (serves 4)

A thick and sumptuous sauce with a delectable "cheddar and beer" flavor. Serve it over whole grain toast points which have been topped with steamed broccoli spears and perhaps some mild red onion rings. Impressive!

1½ C (12 oz.) non-alcoholic lager
    beer
½ C water
⅓ C raw cashew pieces
⅓ C unsalted tomato paste
¼ C nutritional yeast flakes
3 T arrowroot or cornstarch
1 T Vegetarian Worcestershire
    Sauce, p. 93
1½ tsp. onion granules
2 cloves garlic, minced,
    or ½ tsp. garlic granules
½ tsp. paprika
½ tsp. mustard powder
¼ tsp. salt
several drops Tabasco sauce

Place all the ingredients in a blender, and process several minutes until completely smooth. Pour into a saucepan and bring to a boil, stirring constantly. Reduce the heat to low, and cook until thick and smooth, stirring constantly. Serve immediately.

Per serving: Calories: 148, Protein: 5 gm., Carbohydrates: 20 gm., Fat: 5 gm.

White Rabbit

Yield: 2 cups

A thick, rich, velvety smooth cheeze sauce. Elegant over steamed vegetables or potato chunks. Also makes a quick topping for English muffins or French bread pizzas. Simply spread bread or muffin halves with a small amount of pizza sauce, cover with a bit of White Rabbit, *add any additional toppings such as chopped green pepper, sliced mushrooms, or onion, and pop under the broiler until lightly browned.*

1 C firm silken tofu, drained and crumbled
1¼ C water
¼ C nutritional yeast flakes
3 T fresh lemon juice
3 T raw cashew pieces
2 T quick-cooking rolled oats
2 tsp. onion granules
1 tsp. salt
¼ tsp. garlic granules
pinch of ground allspice

Place all the ingredients in a blender, and process several minutes until completely smooth. Pour into a saucepan and bring to a boil. Reduce the heat to medium-low, and cook until thick, stirring constantly.

Per ½ cup serving: Calories: 126, Protein: 9 gm., Carbohydrates: 9 gm., Fat: 6 gm.

Sauces, Pestos & Dressings

Unprocessed Cheeze Sauce

Yield: 4 cups

I've often fantasized about a sauce as velvety smooth and cheezy as the one I imagine June Cleaver made for Ward and the boys, but which would also be low enough in fat so I could indulge guilt-free. Well, if you are like me, wait no longer. Here is an all-American cheese sauce that is rich-tasting, soothing, and satisfying. Pour it over broccoli, potatoes, or elbow macaroni to instantly create those Norman Rockwell dreams.

For a filling fondue, serve Unprocessed Cheeze Sauce from a fondue pot accompanied by all your dipping favorites from bread cubes to vegetable wedges, or even fresh, seasonal fruit.

1 medium potato, peeled and
   coarsely chopped
1 medium carrot, scraped and
   coarsely chopped
1 medium onion, coarsely chopped
1 C water

½ C firm silken tofu, drained and
   crumbled
½ C nutritional yeast flakes
2 T fresh lemon juice
1¼ tsp. salt
1 tsp. onion granules
¼ tsp. garlic granules

Place the potato, carrot, onion, and water in a saucepan, and bring to a boil. Cover and reduce the heat to medium. Simmer for about 10 minutes, or until the vegetables are tender. Transfer to a blender along with the remaining ingredients. Process until velvety smooth. Serve immediately or return to a saucepan or fondue pot to keep warm.

Per ½ cup serving: Calories: 61, Protein: 4 gm., Carbohydrates: 9 gm., Fat: 1 gm.

Rich Unprocessed Cheeze Sauce
Add an additional ½ C tofu during processing to make a richer sauce.

Simply Cheezy Sauce

Yield: 3½ cups

A versatile cheeze sauce that is quick and easy to make. Season it with your favorite dried herbs and pour over pasta or potatoes mixed with steamed vegetables for a "fast food" dinner the whole family will enjoy. Also makes a delicious fondue.

3 C water
¼ C quick-cooking rolled oats
⅓ C nutritional yeast flakes
4 T tahini
4 T arrowroot or cornstarch
2 T fresh lemon juice
1 T onion granules
1¼ tsp. salt
1 tsp. dried thyme leaves, basil leaves, oregano leaves, or dill weed
½ tsp. garlic granules
⅛ tsp. turmeric powder
several drops Tabasco sauce, to taste

Place all the ingredients in a blender, and process until completely smooth. Pour into a medium saucepan, and bring to a boil, stirring constantly. Reduce the heat to low, and continue to cook for a few more minutes, stirring constantly, until thick and smooth. Serve hot.

Per ½ cup serving: Calories: 97, Protein: 4 gm., Carbohydrates: 11 gm., Fat: 5 gm.

Tomato Con Queso Sauce

Yield: 3 cups

This sauce is wonderful over pasta, rice, or potatoes, and is particularly gorgeous over blue corn chips. For authentic flavor, add some freshly chopped cilantro to taste.

1 C Gee Whiz spread, p. 19
2 C fat-free salsa

Stir together Gee Whiz Spread and salsa until well combined. Serve at room temperature or heat gently over low in a medium saucepan until warm, stirring constantly.

Per ¼ cup serving: Calories: 54, Protein: 3 gm., Carbohydrates: 8 gm., Fat: 1 gm.

Instant Cheeze Sauce

Yield: 3 cups

This is the quintessential sauce for broccoli, cauliflower, or potatoes.

2 C Gee Whiz Spread, p. 19
1 C low-fat dairy-free (vegan) milk

Place Gee Whiz Spread and milk in a medium saucepan, and stir until well combined. Heat gently over low until warm, stirring constantly.

Per ¼ cup serving: Calories: 90, Protein: 5 gm., Carbohydrates: 13 gm., Fat: 2 gm.

Chili Con Queso Sauce

Add 3 (4 oz.) cans chopped green chilies to *Instant Cheeze Sauce*, and increase onion granules to 1 tsp.

Chilies, Corn & Jack Cheeze

Yield: 2½ cups (serves 4)

This sauce is low in fat but high in flavor, a little spicy, and delectably cheezy. Serve it over rice, baked potatoes, baked tortilla chips, corn bread, or toast. If desired, top each serving with a dollop of Kefir Cheeze, pg. 36, or Tofu Sour Cream, pg. 90.

1½ C water
2 T fresh lemon juice
⅓ C quick-cooking rolled oats
¼ C nutritional yeast flakes
2 T arrowroot or cornstarch
¼ tsp. mustard powder
2 tsp. onion granules
1¼ tsp. salt

¼ C water + 1 T balsamic vinegar,
    fresh lemon juice,
    or non-alcoholic white wine
2 cloves garlic, chopped
1 small onion, chopped
1 (4 oz.) can mild green chilies,
    peeled and chopped
2 C fresh corn kernels,
    or frozen corn kernels, thawed
    under hot tap water and
    drained

Place the water, lemon juice, rolled oats, nutritional yeast flakes, arrowroot or cornstarch, mustard powder, onion granules, and salt in a blender, and process several minutes until very smooth. Set aside.

In a medium saucepan, heat the water and vinegar, lemon juice, or wine, add the garlic and onion, and cook until soft. Stir in the chilies and corn, cover, and cook over medium-low until the corn is tender (about 5-10 minutes). Add a little more water to prevent sticking, if necessary.

Stir in the blended mixture, and cook, stirring often, until thickened (about 8-10 minutes). Serve immediately.

Per serving: Calories: 155, Protein: 6 gm., Carbohydrates: 30 gm., Fat: 0 gm.

Zucchini Fontinella Sauce

Yield: 3½ cups (4 to 6 servings)

A creamy but delicate sauce that is delicious over pasta, grains, Plain Polenta, *pg. 105, or corn bread. Top each serving with a bit of* Parmazano, *pg. 25, if desired.*

1½ C water
2 T fresh lemon juice
⅓ C quick-cooking rolled oats
¼ C nutritional yeast flakes
2 T arrowroot or cornstarch
½ tsp. mustard powder
2 tsp. onion granules
1¼ tsp. salt

2 T water + 1 tsp. balsamic vinegar
    or fresh lemon juice
1 large clove garlic, chopped
4 scallions, sliced
1 large red or green bell pepper,
    chopped
2 medium or 3 small zucchini,
    shredded
2 medium fresh tomatoes, seeded
    and lightly diced
¼ C fresh parsley, chopped,
    or 1 T dried parsley flakes
5 leaves fresh basil, torn,
    or 1 tsp. dried basil leaves
½ tsp. ground nutmeg
freshly ground black pepper, to
    taste

Place the water, lemon juice, rolled oats, nutritional yeast flakes, arrowroot or cornstarch, mustard powder, onion granules, and salt in a blender, and process several minutes until very smooth. Set aside.

Heat the water and vinegar or lemon juice in a large skillet. Add the garlic, scallions, and bell pepper, and cook for 5 minutes. Add the remaining ingredients and cook just until slightly softened (about 2 minutes).

Stir in the blended mixture, and cook, stirring often, until thickened (about 8-10 minutes). Serve immediately.

Per serving: Calories: 81, Protein: 4 gm., Carbohydrates: 14 gm., Fat: 0 gm.

Cheezy Vegetable Béchamel Sauce

Yield: 3 cups (enough for 1 lb. of pasta or 4 servings)

Chunks of crisp vegetables bathed in a cheezy white sauce. Serve over pasta, polenta, couscous, steamed grains, or potatoes with a sprinkling of poppy seeds on top.

⅓ C water + 2 T fresh lemon juice
  or non-alcoholic white wine
1 medium onion, diced
4 cloves garlic, minced
1 medium carrot, thinly sliced on
  diagonal
2 stalks celery, thinly sliced on
  diagonal
1 large green or red bell pepper,
  diced
7 medium mushrooms, thinly sliced
2 scallions, sliced

2 C low-fat, dairy-free (vegan) milk
⅓ C unbleached all-purpose flour
2 T All-Season Blend, p. 93
2 tsp. dried basil leaves
½ tsp. ground fennel seed
⅛ tsp. freshly ground black pepper

Heat the water and lemon juice or wine in a large saucepan. Add the onion, garlic, carrot, celery, and pepper. Cover and cook over medium-high, stirring occasionally, until the carrot is crisp-tender (about 10 minutes). Add the mushrooms and scallions, and cook, uncovered, for 3-5 minutes longer.

Place the remaining ingredients in a blender, and process until smooth. Pour over the vegetables and stir to mix well. Cook over medium, stirring almost constantly, until thickened (about 10 minutes). Serve immediately.

Per serving: Calories: 132, Protein: 4 gm., Carbohydrates: 26 gm., Fat: 1 gm.

Southwestern Beer & Longhorn Sauce

Yield: 4 cups (8 servings)

This sauce is thick and hearty with chunks of tomatoes and peppers. It is delicious rolled in flour or corn tortillas or poured over tortilla chips, hearty grains or potatoes, and any dish containing beans. It is also a great hot dip or fondue. For a party appetizer, cut off the top of a medium-sized, crusty, round loaf of bread, and scoop out the soft middle. Cut the top and removed bread into cubes. Serve the hot sauce in the center of the bread bowl with the cubed bread on the side to dunk into it.

¼ C water + 1 T fresh lemon juice
   or balsamic vinegar
1 medium onion, chopped
3 cloves garlic, finely chopped or
   pressed

1 large green bell pepper, chopped
2 fresh, ripe tomatoes, coarsely
   chopped
1 tsp. ground cumin
1 tsp. ground coriander
¼ tsp. Tabasco sauce, or to taste
¼ tsp. freshly ground black pepper
1-2 tsp. sweetener of your choice
   (optional)
1½ C (12 oz.) non-alcoholic lager
   beer

Heat the water and lemon juice or vinegar in a large saucepan. Add the onion and garlic; cover and cook until the onion is translucent. Stir in the pepper, tomatoes, seasonings, and sweetener; cover and cook over medium for 10 minutes, stirring often. Stir in the beer and simmer, uncovered, for 20 minutes, stirring often.

...continued on next page

1½ C water
½ C pimiento pieces, drained
⅓ C quick-cooking rolled oats
¼ C nutritional yeast flakes
¼ C unbleached all-purpose flour
   or whole wheat pastry flour
3 T fresh lemon juice
2 T arrowroot or cornstarch
1 T onion granules
1 tsp. salt
¼ tsp. mustard powder

Meanwhile, place the remaining ingredients in a blender, and process several minutes until completely smooth. Pour the blended liquid into the vegetable/beer mixture, and cook over medium-low, stirring constantly, until very thick and hot (about 10 minutes).

Per serving: Calories: 76, Protein: 3 gm., Carbohydrates: 14 gm., Fat: 0 gm

Walnut Gjetost Sauce

Yield: 2⅓ cups (8 servings)

Simple ingredients meld to create an absolutely heavenly flavor. Rich but delicate.

1 C walnut pieces

1½ C water
4 T sweet white miso
3 T mirin

Place the walnuts on a dry cookie sheet or in a toaster oven at 350°F, and roast for 12-15 minutes, or until lightly browned and fragrant; cool. Place in a blender or food processor with the remaining ingredients, and process several minutes until completely smooth. Serve at room temperature over hot grains or vegetables.

Per serving: Calories: 118, Protein: 3 gm., Carbohydrates: 5 gm., Fat: 9 gm.

Pecan Gjetost Sauce

Substitute 1 C pecan pieces for the walnuts, and eliminate the mirin.

Creamy Pesto Dip, Topping & Spread

Yield: 2½ cups

Pesto is a delectable topping typically containing pine nuts, lots of olive oil, fresh basil, plenty of garlic, and Parmesan cheese. Most often it is used as a topping or condiment for pasta. In the following recipe, the oil has been replaced with silken tofu, walnuts substitute for the more pricey pine nuts, and nutritional yeast stands in for the Parmesan cheese. Nevertheless, the flavor is amazingly authentic.

This pesto is delicious in its traditional role as a pasta topper, but it is also terrific as a condiment for steamed rice or vegetables and is especially wonderful on baked potatoes. It is a very thick topping so you may want to thin it with a bit of low-fat, dairy-free (vegan) milk when using it as a sauce. However, because of its thickness, this pesto is versatile enough to be used as a dip for crackers and veggies or as a tasty spread for sandwiches. Serve it at room temperature when using with pasta or grains, or serve it room temperature or chilled for dipping or spreading.

1 C walnuts

1 (10.5 oz.) pkg. firm silken tofu, drained and crumbled
1 C fresh basil or cilantro leaves, lightly packed
6 T nutritional yeast flakes
¼ C water
2 T fresh lemon juice
3-4 small cloves garlic, chopped or pressed
¾ tsp. salt

Place the walnuts on a dry baking sheet, and toast in a 350°F oven or toaster oven until lightly browned, about 10 minutes. If you prefer, toast the walnuts in a dry skillet instead until lightly browned and fragrant, stirring constantly.

Place the toasted walnuts and remaining ingredients in a food processor, and process until smooth. Serve at room temperature or chilled.

Per 2 Tbsp. serving: Calories: 60, Protein: 3 gm., Carbohydrates: 3 gm., Fat: 4 gm.

Spinach Tomato Pesto

Yield: 2⅔ cups

An absolutely exquisite pesto, yet very simple to prepare. Equally great as a dip or topping served at room temperature, or as a warm sauce over pasta or rice.

1½ C water
1 (10 oz.) pkg. frozen chopped
    spinach, cooked and drained
    well
½ C fresh parsley, chopped and
    lightly packed
½ C fresh basil leaves, lightly
    packed
½ C pine nuts
1 (6 oz.) can unsalted tomato paste
¼ C nutritional yeast flakes
4-6 cloves garlic, chopped
½ tsp. salt

Place all the ingredients in a blender, and process several minutes into a thick purée. Serve at room temperature, or transfer to a saucepan and heat over medium-low until just warmed through.

Per ⅓ cup serving: Calories: 94, Protein: 5 gm., Carbohydrates: 9 gm., Fat: 5 gm.

Eggplant Pecan Pesto

Yield: about 3 cups

This enchanting pesto is stupendous as a hot dip, warm spread, or a thick pasta topping. If a thinner sauce is preferred, add a little water to achieve the desired consistency.

½ C water, or more as needed
1 medium onion, diced
4 cloves garlic, chopped

1 large eggplant, peeled

1 C pecans
¼ C fresh basil leaves, lightly
   packed
3 T fresh lemon juice
2 T sweet white miso

In a large skillet, heat the water and cook the onion and garlic over medium-high for 5 minutes.

Meanwhile, peel the eggplant and cut it into ½-inch cubes. Add the eggplant to the onion, cover, and reduce the heat to medium. Cook, stirring often until the eggplant is very soft, about 25-30 minutes. If necessary, add a little more water to prevent the eggplant from sticking to the pan.

When the eggplant is tender, transfer the mixture to a blender. Add the remaining ingredients and process until puréed and completely smooth. The mixture will be very thick. Serve immediately while warm. It may also be served at room temperature or stored in the refrigerator and reheated.

Per ¼ cup serving: Calories: 86, Protein: 1 gm., Carbohydrates: 7 gm., Fat: 6 gm.

Mornay Sauce

Yield: 3½ cups

A rich, versatile, lightly cheesy white sauce that is amazingly easy to prepare.

3 C water
½ C raw cashew pieces
⅓ C nutritional yeast flakes
¼ C fresh lemon juice
4 T arrowroot or cornstarch
2 tsp. onion granules
1 tsp. garlic granules
1 tsp. salt

2 tsp. Vegetarian Worcestershire
    Sauce, p. 93
1 tsp. Dijon mustard
dash of freshly grated nutmeg,
    or ground nutmeg

Process the first eight ingredients in a blender until smooth and creamy. Pour into a medium saucepan, and bring to a boil, stirring constantly. Reduce the heat to low, and cook until thick and smooth, stirring constantly.

Remove from the heat and stir in the remaining ingredients. Serve immediately.

Per ½ cup serving: Calories: 100, Protein: 4 gm., Carbohydrates: 10 gm., Fat: 5 gm.

"Say Cheeze" Gravy

Yield: 2½ cups

A quick, wonderful gravy for mashed potatoes or biscuits, or for making potatoes and cheeze, vegetable and cheeze goulash, and more. It stores well in the refrigerator for several days, but will thicken as it cools. If it becomes too thick for your liking, simply whisk in a tablespoon or two of additional water, non-alcoholic wine, or dairy-free (vegan) milk when you reheat it.

1½ C low-fat, dairy-free (vegan) milk
1 C water
½ C unbleached all-purpose flour
   or whole wheat pastry flour
½ C nutritional yeast flakes
2 T tamari
2 T mirin, sherry, or non-alcoholic
   wine
¾ tsp. salt
pinch of ground white pepper

Blend all the ingredients until very smooth and creamy. Pour into a saucepan and bring to a boil, stirring constantly. Reduce the heat to low and cook, beating constantly with a wire whisk, until thick, hot, and bubbly (about 5 minutes). Stir in the mirin and serve immediately.

Per ½ cup serving: Calories: 120, Protein: 8 gm., Carbohydrates: 19 gm., Fat: 1 gm.

Cold Mostarella Sauce

Yield: 1⅔ cups (serves 6)

This sauce is remarkably adaptable. Not too thick, not too thin—like a luscious, dairy-free, pourable mozzarella. Great on hot or cold pasta, vegetable salads, or steamed grains and vegetables. Also delicious as a dressing for raw salad greens.

1 C water
¼ C raw cashew pieces
¼ C raw sesame seeds*
3 T nutritional yeast flakes
3 T fresh lemon juice
2 tsp. onion granules
¾ tsp. salt
¼ tsp. garlic granules

Place all the ingredients in a blender, and process several minutes until smooth and creamy. Store in the refrigerator.

Per serving: Calories: 87, Protein: 3 gm., Carbohydrates: 6 gm., Fat: 6 gm.

If raw sesame seeds are not available, an equal amount of tahini may be substituted but will result in a smoother, less "toothy" sauce.

Cold Provolone Cheeze Sauce

Make *Cold Mostarella Sauce*, reducing the nutritional yeast to 2 T. Use 2 tsp. hickory smoked (Bakon) nutritional yeast, or ¼ tsp. liquid smoke, or 1 tsp. hickory salt and only ¼ tsp. table salt.

Tangy Chedda Sauce

Yield: 2 cups (serves 8)

*Serve cold over split baked potatoes topped with veggies, over baked tortilla chips
as a quick "nacho" topping, or use your favorite salsa in place of the water and pimientos,
and add some chopped, fresh cilantro for an unbeatable cold "con queso" sauce.*

1 C water
½ C pimiento pieces, drained
¼ C raw cashew pieces
¼ C raw sesame seeds*
¼ C nutritional yeast flakes
3 T fresh lemon juice
2 tsp. onion granules
¾ tsp. salt
¼ tsp. garlic granules
¼ tsp. ground dill seed
⅛ tsp. ground allspice

Place all the ingredients in a blender, and process several minutes until smooth and creamy. Store in the refrigerator.

For a *Hot Chedda Sauce*, warm over medium heat, stirring constantly, until hot, thickened, and bubbly.

Per serving: Calories: 73, Protein: 3 gm., Carbohydrates: 6 gm., Fat: 4 gm.

If raw sesame seeds are not available, an equal amount of tahini may be substituted but will result in a smoother, less "toothy" sauce.

Egg-Free (Vegan) Mayonnaise

Yield: 1⅔ cups

Mayonnaise is a rich, high-fat dressing that typically is made with raw eggs, egg yolks, and a lot of oil. The following recipe is much lower in fat but just as tasty as conventional mayonnaise. Use it on sandwiches, in recipes, and wherever you would consider using regular mayonnaise.

1 (10.5 oz.) pkg. firm silken tofu,
    drained and crumbled
2 T fresh lemon juice
1 T white wine vinegar,
    or brown rice vinegar
1-2 tsp. brown rice syrup,
    or sweetener of your choice
1 tsp. salt
1 tsp. prepared yellow mustard

Process all the ingredients in a blender until smooth and creamy. Store in the refrigerator.

Per 2 Tbsp. serving: Calories: 21, Protein: 2 gm., Carbohydrates: 1 gm., Fat: 1 gm.

Rich and Creamy Egg-Free Mayonnaise

For an even richer, creamier mayonnaise, 2-3 T of canola oil may be added during processing, if desired.

Tofu Sour Cream

Yield: 1½ cups

This non-dairy, sour cream substitute is just as flavorful and versatile as its dairy counterpart and a snap to prepare, even at the last minute. Try adding some fresh or dried dill weed for a tasty baked potato topping or some snipped chives, dried onion flakes, and a bit of garlic powder to create the ever popular "onion dip" for chips.

1 (10.5 oz.) pkg. silken tofu, drained
    and crumbled
2 T canola oil (optional)
1 T fresh lemon juice
1 T brown rice vinegar
1 tsp. brown rice syrup
½ tsp. apple cider vinegar
½ tsp. salt

Process all the ingredients for several minutes in a blender or food processor until completely smooth. Store in the refrigerator.

Per 2 Tbsp. serving: Calories: 21, Protein: 2 gm.,
Carbohydrates: 1 gm., Fat: 1 gm.

Walnut Chèvre Dressing

Yield: 1⅔ cups (6 servings)

A smooth, rich dressing with a subtle but sublime flavor.

1 C low-fat, dairy-free (vegan) milk
½ C walnut pieces
3 T nutritional yeast flakes
3 T fresh lime juice
2 tsp. tamari
1 tsp. brown rice syrup
1 tsp. dried basil leaves
¼ tsp. dried marjoram leaves
1 clove garlic, chopped

Place all the ingredients in a blender, and process until completely smooth.

Per serving: Calories: 98, Protein: 4 gm.,
Carbohydrates: 7 gm., Fat: 6 gm.

Green Goddess Ranch Dressing

Yield: 2¼ cups

Far superior to store-bought ranch brands, this cream-cheezy dressing is a family favorite and fortunately quite simple to make from scratch.

1½ C low-fat, dairy-free (vegan) milk
1 T umeboshi plum paste
3 T tahini
2 T fresh parsley, chopped
1 scallion, sliced
1 tsp. dried tarragon leaves
1-2 cloves garlic, pressed
pinch of ground white pepper
    (optional)

Place all the ingredients in a blender, and process until smooth and creamy.

Per ¼ cup serving: Calories: 44, Protein: 1 gm., Carbohydrates: 4 gm., Fat: 2 gm.

Marinara Sauce

Yield: about 6 cups

This fairly simple tomato sauce is surprisingly flavorful and hearty—especially if allowed to chill overnight to permit flavors to marry. It is the ideal sauce to accompany spaghetti, Nino's Manicotti, pg. 154, or any of our cheeze croquette recipes.

5 cloves garlic, finely chopped
1 small onion, diced
¼ C non-alcoholic wine,
    or 3 T water + 1 T balsamic
    vinegar or mirin
¼ tsp. crushed red pepper flakes
2 (6 oz.) cans unsalted tomato paste
1 (28 oz.) can Italian pear tomatoes,
    coarsely chopped, with juice
    (about 4 cups)
1⅓ C water
½-1 tsp. sweetener of your choice
½ tsp. salt, or to taste
⅛ tsp. freshly ground black pepper
1 tsp. dried oregano leaves
2 T fresh parsley,* finely chopped
5 large leaves fresh basil,* finely
    chopped

In a large saucepan, cook the onion and garlic in the wine or water and vinegar, covered, until tender, about 10 minutes. Add the pepper flakes and cook, uncovered, for 1 minute. Add the tomato paste and cook, stirring constantly, for 1 minute. Then add the tomatoes and their juice, water, sweetener, salt, pepper, and oregano. Simmer, uncovered, for 30-45 minutes, stirring often. Add the fresh herbs during the last 10 minutes of cooking.

If a smoother sauce is preferred, force the mixture through a food mill or strainer prior to adding the fresh herbs. Return the purée to the cooking pot, and add the herbs. Cook for 10 minutes longer.

If possible, allow the sauce to chill in the refrigerator overnight to permit the flavors to blend.

Per 1 cup serving: Calories: 84, Protein: 3 gm., Carbohydrates: 17 gm., Fat: 0 gm.

*If fresh herbs are not available, substitute dried herbs using 2 tsp. dried parsley flakes and 1 tsp. dried basil leaves and add them along with the tomatoes.

All-Season Blend

Yield: 1¼ cups

*This is an excellent all-purpose seasoning for sauces, gravies, and even instant soup broth.**

1½ C nutritional yeast flakes
3 T salt
1 T onion granules
1 T paprika
2 tsp. garlic granules
1 tsp. dried parsley flakes
½ tsp. turmeric
¼ tsp. dried thyme leaves
¼ tsp. dried marjoram leaves
¼ tsp. ground dill seed

Place all the ingredients in a blender or food processor, and process until finely ground. Store in a covered container at room temperature.

*For broth, combine 1½ teaspoons All-Season Blend and 1 cup of water in a small saucepan. (Quantities are easily doubled, tripled, or quadrupled.) Bring to a boil, simmer for 1 minute, and serve.

Per 1 Tbsp. serving: Calories: 30, Protein: 4 gm., Carbohydrates: 4 gm., Fat: 0 gm.

Vegetarian Worcestershire Sauce

Yield: 1½ cups

No anchovies!

6 T water
6 T brown rice syrup
¼ C tamari
2 T apple cider vinegar
1 tsp. barley malt syrup
1 tsp. ground ginger
¼ tsp. garlic granules
⅛ tsp. cayenne pepper
tiny pinch ground cloves
tiny pinch onion granules

Place all the ingredients in a blender, bowl, or jar with a lid. Blend, whisk, or shake until the mixture is smooth and the powders are well incorporated. Store in the refrigerator; this keeps well.

Per Tbsp. serving: Calories: 10, Protein: 0 gm., Carbohydrates: 2 gm., Fat: 0 gm.

Pizzas, Polentas & Breads

Deep-Dish Vegetable Pizza

Yield: one 14-inch deep-dish pizza or two 9-inch deep-dish pizzas (8 servings)

Make this when you have a little extra time to spare. It's one of the most delicious pizzas of any kind I've ever eaten, and certainly worth the effort. If you make the sauce and "cheezes" a day or so in advance, the final assembly will actually be quite easy.

Crust

1 T (1 pkg.) active dry yeast (for baking)
1 C lukewarm water (105°F to 115°F)
½-1 tsp. sweetener of your choice
1 tsp. salt
3-4 C whole wheat bread flour (or part unbleached white bread flour)

Lightly oil one 14-inch deep-dish pizza pan or two 9-inch layer-cake pans, and set aside.

In a large bowl, soften the yeast in ¼ cup of the lukewarm water, and allow to rest for about 5 minutes. Stir in the sweetener, salt, and remaining water. Gradually stir in the flour, beating vigorously until no more flour can be incorporated. Turn out onto a well-floured board and knead for 5-10 minutes, adding additional flour as necessary. Form into a ball and place in an oiled bowl, turning the dough to coat. Drape the bowl with a damp cloth, and let the dough rise in a warm place for 45 minutes to 1 hour, until doubled.

When the dough is finished rising, punch down and knead lightly in the bowl. Turn the dough out onto a floured board. Roll into an 18-inch circle (to fit a 14-inch deep-dish pizza pan), or divide the dough in half, and roll each half into a 12-inch circle (for two 9-inch deep-dish pizza pans). Place the dough into the pan, and roll the edge over to form a finished rim.

Fifteen minutes before baking, place a rack in the center of the oven, and preheat the oven to 425°F. Prick the dough in several places with a fork, and bake until very lightly browned, about 5-10 minutes, to set the gluten. Let cool for 5 minutes before adding the sauce and remaining toppings and returning to the oven for baking.

...continued on next page

Spicy Vegetable Sauce

(may be prepared a day or two in advance and stored in the refrigerator)

2 (16 oz.) cans or 1 (32 oz.) can
  unsalted plum tomatoes,
  drained
1 (6 oz.) can unsalted tomato paste
1 T dried basil leaves
2 tsp. dried oregano leaves
1-2 tsp. sweetener of your choice
1 tsp. crushed red pepper flakes
1 tsp. salt

2 T water + 1 T balsamic vinegar or
  fresh lemon juice
1 small onion, chopped
1 large clove garlic, pressed
12 large mushrooms, thinly sliced
2 medium carrots, or 1 large carrot,
  shredded or grated
1 medium zucchini, julienned
½ C black olives, sliced

Place the tomatoes, tomato paste, basil, oregano, sweetener, peppers, and salt in a blender, and process or pulse very briefly, just until well combined but the tomatoes are still a bit chunky. Set aside.

Heat the water and vinegar or lemon juice in a large skillet. Cook the onion and garlic until slightly softened, about 5 minutes. Add the mushrooms and cook over medium-high, stirring often, until almost all of the moisture has evaporated (about 15 minutes). Add the carrots and zucchini, and cook until just softened, about 5 minutes longer.

Stir in the sauce from the blender and the olives, and heat over medium-low until just warmed through, stirring often. Set aside.

Herb Topping

1½ tsp. dried oregano leaves
1½ tsp. dried basil leaves
½ tsp. garlic granules
¼ tsp. freshly ground black pepper

Stir together the dried oregano and basil, the garlic granules, and the black pepper in a small bowl and set aside.

...continued on next page

Mostarella Cheeze Sauce

(may be prepared a day or two in advance and stored in the refrigerator)

1 C water
2 T fresh lemon juice
2 T tahini
¼ C nutritional yeast flakes
3 T quick-cooking rolled oats
1 T arrowroot or cornstarch
⅛ tsp. mustard powder
1½ tsp. onion granules
½ tsp. salt

Have ready:

¼ C Parmazano, p. 25

Place all the ingredients in a blender, and process until the oats are finely ground and the sauce is completely smooth. Pour into a small saucepan, and cook over medium heat until very thick and smooth, stirring constantly. Cover and set aside.

To assemble, spread the vegetable sauce over the cooled crust, leaving a ½-inch rim of crust exposed. Sprinkle on the herb topping.

Spread the cheeze sauce mixture over the sauce and herb topping, distributing it as evenly as possible, then sprinkle the top with Parmazano. Bake for 25-30 minutes at 425°F, or until the bottom of the crust is a deep golden brown. Let rest for 10-15 minutes before slicing.

Per serving: Calories: 324, Protein: 14 gm., Carbohydrates: 56 gm., Fat: 5 gm.

Thin Crust Pizza

Yield: two 12-inch flat round pizzas (8 servings)

This is a traditional, "American-style" pizza, ready to be embellished with all your favorite trimmings. You can use the toppings we have listed here, or you can try adding slices of pepperoni-flavored seitan, grated tempeh, or wheels of tofu sausages. If you are in a hurry and have fresh or frozen, dairy-free pizza shells handy, use the following pizza sauce, cheeze sauce, and your choice of toppings to create a wholesome, "fast food" meal.

Crust
1 T (1 pkg.) active dry yeast (for baking)
½ C plus 2 T warm water (105°F to 115°F)
½-1 tsp. sweetener of your choice
¾ tsp. salt
2-2½ C unbleached white bread flour (or part whole wheat bread flour)

Pizza Sauce
1 C unsalted tomato purée
¼ C water
1½ tsp. dried basil leaves
1½ tsp. dried oregano leaves
1 tsp. onion granules
½ tsp. sweetener of your choice
½ tsp. garlic granules
½ tsp. salt, optional
2-3 cloves garlic, finely chopped

Lightly oil two 12-inch flat, round, pizza pans (or use non-stick pans), and set aside.

Preheat the oven to 425°F. To make the crust, use the ingredients listed here, and follow the directions for *Deep-Dish Vegetable Pizza* crust, pg. 95. Roll the dough into two 13-inch circles. Use a soft pastry brush to remove excess flour. Fold each circle in half, then in quarters, and place in the prepared baking pan with the point of the dough in the center. Unfold the dough and roll the edge over to form a finished rim. Prick the dough all over with a fork. Bake for 3-4 minutes until very lightly brown. Remove from the oven and let cool. Turn the oven temperature up to 450°F.

Stir together all the pizza sauce ingredients. Let the sauce rest while preparing the remaining ingredients to permit the flavors to blend.

...continued on next page

Cheeze Sauce

½ C water
2 T fresh lemon juice
2 T tahini
2 T nutritional yeast flakes
2 T quick-cooking rolled oats
2 tsp. arrowroot or cornstarch
1 tsp. onion granules
¼ tsp. salt

Optional Vegetable Toppings

(use half of total amount for each pizza)

1 C mushrooms, thinly sliced
1 C red or green bell pepper, diced
½ to 1 C onion, chopped
½ to 1 C carrot, grated

Have ready:
¼ C Parmazano, p. 25

Place all the ingredients for the cheeze sauce in a blender, and process until the oats are finely ground and the sauce is completely smooth. Set aside.

To assemble the pizzas, spread the pizza sauce thinly over each cooled crust, leaving a ½-inch rim of crust exposed.

Drizzle half the cheeze sauce evenly over each pizza, and sprinkle the tops equally with the Parmazano. Top with vegetable toppings, if desired.

Bake at 450°F for about 8 minutes, or until the bottom of the crusts are a deep golden brown.

Per serving: Calories: 197, Protein: 9 gm., Carbohydrates: 34 gm., Fat: 3 gm.

Calzones

Yield: 6 calzones

Calzones are essentially individual pizzas with the filling on the inside of the crust instead of on top. Below is the recipe for the standard dough, along with instructions for assembling and baking. To maximize your time, prepare your filling while the dough is rising. Serve plain or with Marinara Sauce, pg. 92.

1½ tsp. active dry yeast (for baking)
½-1 tsp. sweetener of your choice
1 C lukewarm water
¾ tsp. salt
1½ C unbleached white bread flour
1-1½ C whole wheat bread flour
additional flour, as necessary, for
    kneading

1 lb. fresh spinach, cooked, drained
    and chopped,
    or 1 (10 oz.) pkg. frozen chopped
    spinach, cooked and drained

¼ C water
1 T balsamic vinegar or fresh lemon
    juice
½ C onion, chopped
2 cloves garlic, pressed

Place the yeast, sweetener, and water in a large bowl, and let rest until foamy, about 5 minutes.

Stir in the salt and flours. Turn out on a floured board, and knead for 10-15 minutes, until smooth and elastic. Place in an oiled bowl, turning the dough to coat. Drape the bowl with a damp towel, and let the dough rise in a warm place until doubled, about 1 hour.

Meanwhile, prepare the spinach/ricotta filling by placing the cooked spinach in a wire mesh strainer and pressing firmly with a fork or the back of a spoon to express as much liquid as possible. Set aside.

Heat the water and vinegar or lemon juice in a small skillet, and cook the onion and garlic until crisp-tender, about 10 minutes. Place in a bowl and stir in the remaining ingredients, including the spinach and Parmazano. Mix thoroughly; this may take a few minutes in order to distribute all the ingredients evenly. Set aside.

Preheat the oven to 400°F.

...continued on next page

1 lb. firm regular tofu, well mashed
3 T fresh lemon juice
2 tsp. dried basil leaves
1 tsp. onion granules
½ tsp. garlic granules
pinch of freshly grated nutmeg,
   or ground nutmeg
freshly ground black pepper,
   to taste

Have ready:

½ C Parmazano, p. 25

Punch down the dough and divide into six equal balls. Roll out each ball on a floured board into a 6-inch round. Fill with a heaping ½ cup of filling, placing the filling on one half of the round only, and leaving a ½-inch rim. Lightly moisten the rim with water, and fold the empty side of the dough over the filled side. Flute the edges or dip a fork in flour and crimp the edges to seal, then prick the dough in several places on the top. Place on a lightly oiled or non-stick baking sheet, and bake for 25-30 minutes, until golden brown.

Per calzone: Calories: 335, Protein: 18 gm., Carbohydrates: 52 gm., Fat: 5 gm.

Focaccia

Yield: 8-10 servings

Focaccia is a thin, cracker-like Italian bread. You can vary the toppings by replacing the one that I suggest with an Uncheese pesto, or perhaps a mixture of seeded and sliced fresh plum tomatoes or red bell pepper strips, and artichoke hearts. If desired, sprinkle lightly with Parmazano, pg. 25, after removing the focaccia from the oven. Simply think of this bread as a wafer-thin pizza crust, and use your imagination! Not only is this bread delicious and different, it is easy to make and bakes exceptionally quickly.

½ C tomato juice (salted or
    unsalted)
¼ C onion, minced,
    or 5 cloves garlic, minced
1½ tsp. poppy seeds
¼ tsp. crushed red pepper flakes

2 tsp. active dry yeast (for baking)
1 C lukewarm water
½ tsp. salt

2½-3 C whole wheat bread flour
additional flour as necessary, for
    kneading

To make the topping, combine the first four ingredients in a small bowl, and set side.

Place the yeast and water in a large bowl, and let stand for 5 minutes. Stir in the salt and 1½ cups of the flour; beat well. Gradually stir in the remaining flour until no more flour can be incorporated. Turn out onto a lightly floured board, and knead for about 10 minutes, adding additional flour as necessary to achieve a smooth, elastic dough. Form into a ball and place in an oiled bowl, turning the dough to coat. Drape the bowl with a damp cloth, and let the dough rise in a warm spot until doubled, about an hour.

...continued on next page

About 15 minutes before baking, place a rack in the center of the oven, and preheat the oven to 425°F. Punch down the dough and place on a lightly floured board. Roll into a rectangle about 9" x 13". Place in an oiled or non-stick baking pan lightly sprinkled with cornmeal. (Use a pan at least 9" x 13" in size or larger; the larger your pan, the thinner and crispier the bread will be.) Gently stretch and press the dough to fit the bottom.

Spread the reserved topping mixture over the dough to within ½ inch of the edge. Bake for 5 minutes. Remove from the oven and use a fork to pierce the air bubbles on the surface. Return to the oven and bake until golden brown, about 20-25 minutes longer. Remove from the pan and cut into eight equal pieces. This is best if eaten hot, but is also great at room temperature.

Per serving: Calories: 132, Protein: 5 gm., Carbohydrates: 26 gm., Fat: 0 gm.

Chedda & Onion Pan Bread

Yield: one 9" x 13" pan bread or two 8-inch pan breads (8 servings)

Flavorful bread and cheeze squares. Almost a main dish in itself, this is an excellent accompaniment to hot or cold seasonal salads or soups. Best if served warm. Store leftovers in the refrigerator and reheat in the oven or toaster oven.

½ C onion, chopped
2 T water
½ tsp. dill weed
½ tsp. paprika

Prepare the dough as for *Thin Crust Pizza*, pg. 98. Lightly oil a 9" x 13" pan or two 8-inch square pans, and press in the dough to cover the bottom, taking care not to stretch or tear it. Drape with a damp towel, and let the dough rise again for 40-60 minutes. Bake in a preheated 425°F oven for 5 minutes to set the gluten. Remove from the oven and allow to cool while preparing the topping.

Prepare ½ recipe *Tangy Chedda Sauce*, pg. 88, using tahini instead of sesame seeds and replacing the dill seed and allspice with ⅛ tsp. mustard powder.

Heat the water in a medium saucepan, add the onion, cover, and cook until tender (about 10 minutes). Stir the *Chedda Sauce* into the onions along with dill weed and paprika. Cook over medium heat, stirring often, until thickened, about 8-10 minutes.

Spread the sauce evenly over the dough. For a pizza-type effect, a topping of sliced olives and thinly sliced fresh, ripe tomatoes can be added. Return to the oven and bake for 20-25 minutes. Cut into 2" x 4" pieces to serve.

Per serving: Calories: 165, Protein: 5 gm., Carbohydrates: 29 gm., Fat: 3 gm.

Plain Polenta

Yield: 1½ cups (4 servings)

A basic Italian staple, traditionally served with a tomato sauce, vegetables, or cheese.

1 C coarse, whole grain cornmeal
½ tsp. salt
3 C water

In a medium saucepan, mix together the cornmeal, salt, and 1 cup of the water to make a smooth paste. Gradually stir in the remaining water. Bring to a boil, stirring constantly. Lower the heat and simmer, stirring often, for 30-45 minutes, or until the mixture is very thick but not stiff, and begins to pull away from the sides of the pan.

Per serving: Calories: 125, Protein: 3 gm., Carbohydrates: 27 gm., Fat: 0 gm.

Italian Cheeze Polenta

This is especially good with Marinara Sauce, *pg. 92, and vegetables—try zucchini, cauliflower, broccoli, or green beans.*

Prepare 1 recipe of *Plain Polenta*, omitting the salt. When the polenta is finished cooking, beat in ½ C Parmazano, p. 25, and serve immediately.

Mammaliga

This is a satisfying, peasant-style polenta with cheeze. Serve it with fresh tomatoes and a hearty rye or pumpernickel bread.

Prepare 1 recipe of *Plain Polenta*. Divide it among four serving bowls, and top each portion with 2 T *Tofu Ricotta*, pg. 27, drained *Betta Feta*, pg. 28, or *Roquefort Dip & Dressing*, pg. 24. Toss on a few sliced olives and sprinkle with fresh or dried dill weed.

Cornmeal Pie With Monterey Jack

Yield: one 9-inch or 10-inch pie (6 servings)

A polenta-crusted pizza! This recipe involves several steps, and the crust must be prepared in advance, but none of the steps is complicated or difficult to do. And the results are well worth the small amount of extra time and effort.

Initially follow the recipe below. Then, next time try ½ cup thinly sliced mushrooms instead of, or in addition to, the bell pepper, or add some olives, garlic, or whatever else inspires you!

Have ready:

1 recipe Plain Polenta, p. 105

¾ C water
3 T quick-cooking rolled oats
3 T nutritional yeast flakes
2 T fresh lemon juice
2 T tahini
1 T arrowroot or cornstarch
1½ tsp. onion granules
½ tsp. salt
¼ tsp. mustard powder

For a cornmeal crust, prepare 1 recipe *Plain Polenta*, pg. 105. Lightly oil a 9-inch or 10-inch pie plate. Spoon in the polenta and spread it evenly into a thick crust. Refrigerate it or cool it at room temperature for ½ hour or longer to firm it up. (The cooled crust may be covered and refrigerated overnight, if preferred.) Bake the cooled crust in a 400°F oven for 45-50 minutes.

To make a Monterey Jack topping, place the next nine ingredients in a blender, and process until the oats are finely ground and the sauce is completely smooth. Pour into a saucepan and cook over medium, stirring constantly, until very thick and smooth (about 8-10 minutes). Cover and set aside.

...continued on next page

⅓ C water

1½ T balsamic vinegar, fresh lemon juice, or non-alcoholic white wine

1 medium onion, thinly sliced

2 cloves garlic, minced

1 red or green bell pepper, finely chopped

½ tsp. dried oregano leaves

freshly ground black pepper, to taste

1 medium, fresh, ripe tomato, sliced

Have ready:

⅓ C Parmazano, p. 25

While the crust is baking, prepare a vegetable filling by braising the onion, garlic, and pepper in the water and vinegar, lemon juice, or wine in a covered saucepan until tender (about 10-15 minutes) . Stir in the oregano and black pepper, and set aside. Slice the tomato thinly and set aside.

Preheat the oven to 400°F.

To assemble, spread the vegetable filling over the baked crust, and then arrange the tomato slices over them. Top with the Monterey Jack topping, spreading and distributing it as evenly as possible. Sprinkle the Parmazano evenly over all.

Bake for 15 minutes, or until lightly browned. Let rest 15 minutes before slicing into wedges and serving.

Per serving: Calories: 176, Protein: 6 gm., Carbohydrates: 29 gm., Fat: 3 gm.

Cornmeal Cheeze Pudding

Yield: 2 cups (4 servings)

Serve this glorious, savory pudding in individual bowls topped with your choice of steamed vegetables and perhaps tomato sauce. This is an unusual, soothing, and satisfying main dish that both children and adults delight in. It is also exceptionally easy to make and extremely versatile.

2 C low-fat, dairy-free (vegan) milk
½ C pimiento pieces, drained
¼ C nutritional yeast flakes
2 T fresh lemon juice
2 tsp. onion granules
1 tsp. salt
¾ tsp. mustard powder
½ tsp. garlic granules

1 C coarse, whole grain cornmeal
1 C low-fat, dairy-free (vegan) milk

Place the first eight ingredients in a blender, and process until very smooth. Set aside.

In a medium saucepan, mix together the cornmeal and 1 more cup of the milk to make a smooth paste. Gradually stir in the blended ingredients.

Bring to a boil, stirring constantly. Reduce the heat to low. Cover and cook, stirring often, for 30 minutes. Serve immediately.

Per serving: Calories: 230, Protein: 9 gm., Carbohydrates: 44 gm., Fat: 2 gm.

Corn & Colby Griddle Cakes

Yield: 24 cakes (8 servings)

Cheesy cornmeal pancakes that are light, delicate, and gluten-free! Great by themselves or topped with Tofu Sour Cream, pg. 90, and tomato slices.

¾ C water
¼ C raw cashew pieces
¼ C pimiento pieces, drained
2 T fresh lemon juice
2 T nutritional yeast flakes
1 T tahini
1 tsp. onion granules
½ tsp. salt
⅛ tsp. mustard powder

1 C whole grain yellow cornmeal
½ C whole wheat pastry flour
½ tsp. baking soda
⅔ C low-fat, dairy-free (vegan) milk
1½ tsp. apple cider vinegar
1 T arrowroot or cornstarch

To make a colby cheeze sauce, place the first nine ingredients in a blender, and process several minutes until completely smooth. Pour into a small saucepan, and cook over medium heat, stirring constantly, until very thick (about 15-20 minutes). Set aside to cool.

To make the griddle cake batter, place the cornmeal, flour, and baking soda in a large mixing bowl, and stir with a dry wire whisk to combine well.

In a glass bowl or large measuring cup, stir together the milk and vinegar. Let sit for about 5 minutes. Stir in the arrowroot or cornstarch, and mix well to dissolve it completely. Then stir in the cooled colby cheeze sauce, and mix until well combined. Make a well in the center of the dry ingredients, and pour in the wet mixture. Combine thoroughly.

Lightly oil a large griddle (non-stick works best) over medium-high. When the griddle is very hot, spoon on the batter using 2 tablespoonfuls for each cake. Carefully turn them over when the bottom is a very deep, golden brown. Cook the second side briefly, just until well browned. Re-oil the griddle as necessary. Keep the cakes warm in a 250°F oven while the remainder cook.

Per serving: Calories: 146, Protein: 4 gm., Carbohydrates: 24 gm., Fat: 4 gm.

Cheeze Straws

Yield: 2 dozen straws

Spicy, cheddar-flavored bread sticks—great to carry along for picnics or snacks.
Serve them with soup, salad, chili, or beans and rice—plain or with salsa or mustard.

1 T (1 pkg.) active dry yeast (for baking)
⅓ C lukewarm water

1¼ C low-fat, dairy-free (vegan) milk
1-2 tsp. sweetener of your choice
½ tsp. salt

¼ C pimiento pieces, drained
2 T nutritional yeast flakes
1 T Dijon mustard
½ tsp. Tabasco sauce
½ tsp. onion granules
¼ tsp. garlic granules

approximately 2-2½ C unbleached white bread flour
approximately 1½ C whole wheat bread flour

additional flour as necessary, for kneading

In a large mixing bowl, dissolve the yeast in the lukewarm water, and let rest for 5 minutes.

Meanwhile, heat the milk, sweetener, and salt until just lukewarm. Remove from the heat and cool, if necessary.

Place the lukewarm milk mixture and the next six ingredients in a blender, and process until completely smooth.

Pour the blended ingredients into the bowl with the yeast; mix well. Gradually add the flour, 1 cup at a time, beating well after each addition. When no more flour can be added, turn the dough out onto a well-floured bread board, and knead for about 10 minutes, adding additional flour to achieve a dough that is smooth and elastic. Form into a ball and place the dough in an oiled bowl, turning the dough to coat all sides evenly. Drape the bowl with a damp cloth, and let the dough rise in a warm place until doubled, about 1 hour.

Fifteen minutes before baking, place a rack in the center of the oven, and preheat the oven to 400°F.

...continued on next page

Punch the dough down and knead briefly in the bowl. Divide the dough in half, then divide each half into 12 equal pieces. (It will be easier to work with only half the dough at a time. Keep the resting portion covered until you are ready to use it.) Roll each piece into a rope about ½-inch thick and 6-8 inches long. Place on lightly oiled or non-stick baking sheets. Cover with oiled waxed paper, and !et rise again for 20 minutes.

Bake for 6 minutes, then carefully turn the straws over, and bake 8-10 minutes longer, or until golden brown. Cool on wire racks.

Per straw: Calories: 82, Protein: 3 gm., Carbohydrates: 16 gm., Fat: 0 gm.

Seeded Cheeze Straws

Roll each straw in sesame seeds, poppy seeds, or caraway seeds before placing on baking sheets.

Onion Cheeze Straws

Lightly steam 1 finely chopped medium onion in a little water, and add it to the dough along with the cooled liquid.

Twisted Cheeze Straws

Twist the ends of each straw in opposite directions two or three times before placing on the baking sheet.

Garlic Toast

Yield: 8 servings

This low-fat version of an all-time favorite makes a delightful accompaniment to soups, salads, or pasta dishes. Slow roasting mellows the garlic's bite, turning it into a divine spread.

2 large bulbs garlic

4 whole grain buns, sliced in half
    and toasted,
    or 8 slices Italian bread,
    toasted
8 tsp. Parmazano, p. 25
paprika

Make a garlic butter by removing any loose, papery outer skin from the garlic. Place the whole bulb, root-side-down, in a small, deep casserole dish or garlic baker. Roast in a preheated 350°F oven, covered, for 1 hour. Remove the cover and bake for 30-45 minutes longer or until very soft. Cool until easy to handle. Carefully slice off the top of the bulb, and holding the bulb in your hand, squeeze out the soft garlic from the cloves.

Spread the toasted bun halves or bread with the warm garlic butter. Sprinkle each piece with 1 tsp. of Parmazano, and garnish lightly with paprika. Serve while warm.

Per serving: Calories: 87, Protein: 4 gm., Carbohydrates: 15 gm., Fat: 1 gm.

Garlic Spread

Mix the warm *Garlic Butter* with 1 C cooked Great Northern beans or other white beans and a pinch of salt. Process in a food processor with a metal blade until smooth. Continue with the directions as above.

Provolone Caraway Biscuits

Yield: one dozen biscuits

1⅓ C low-fat, dairy-free (vegan) milk
1 T nutritional yeast flakes
1 T hickory smoked nutritional yeast,
    ½ tsp. hickory salt (if using
    hickory salt, reduce added salt
    in recipe by ¼ tsp.), or ¼ tsp.
    liquid smoke
1-3 tsp. sweetener of your choice
1 tsp. Dijon mustard
1 tsp. Vegetarian Worcestershire
    Sauce, p. 93
1½ tsp. onion granules
½ tsp. mustard powder
½ tsp. salt

1½ C unbleached all-purpose flour
1⅓ C whole wheat pastry flour
2½ tsp. non-aluminum baking
    powder
½ tsp. baking soda
1 tsp. ground caraway seed
⅛ tsp. freshly ground black pepper

Preheat the oven to 400°F.

Place the first nine ingredients in a blender, and process until completely smooth, or beat vigorously with a wire whisk.

In a large bowl, stir together the remaining dry ingredients. Pour in the blended mixture, and stir everything together until moistened. Do not over-mix.

Drop by rounded spoonfuls onto an oiled or non-stick baking sheet, and bake for 15 minutes or until the bottoms are just barely browned. Cool on racks. Serve warm or at room temperature.

Per biscuit: Calories: 111, Protein: 4 gm., Carbohydrates: 22 gm., Fat: 0 gm.

Chedda Biscuits

Yield: one dozen biscuits

These light and tender biscuits make a scrumptious addition to any meal, especially spicy ones, and are even a welcome breakfast treat. Surprisingly, jam is a pleasant accompaniment.

1 C low-fat, non-dairy (vegan) milk
½ C pimiento pieces, drained
2 T fresh lemon juice
2 T nutritional yeast flakes
1 tsp. onion granules
¼ tsp. mustard powder
¼ tsp. garlic granules

1½ C unbleached all-purpose flour
1½ C whole wheat pastry flour
2 tsp. non-aluminum baking
    powder
1 tsp. dried dill weed
¾ tsp. salt
½ tsp. baking soda

Preheat the oven to 400°F.

Place the first seven ingredients in a blender, and process until completely smooth.

In a large bowl, stir together the remaining dry ingredients. Make a well in the center, and pour in the blended mixture. Stir everything together until moistened. Do not over-mix.

Drop by rounded spoonfuls onto an oiled or non-stick baking sheet, and bake for 15-20 minutes or until the bottoms are just barely browned. Cool on wire racks. Serve warm or at room temperature.

Per biscuit: Calories: 116, Protein: 4 gm., Carbohydrates: 23 gm., Fat: 0 gm.

Spicy Corn & Colby Biscuits

Yield: one dozen biscuits

These well-seasoned drop biscuits are a perfect match for any bean or vegetable combination and are an especially good companion to meals with Mexican, Spanish, or Italian-style seasonings.

1 C low-fat, non-dairy (vegan) milk
½ C pimiento pieces, drained
2 T fresh lemon juice
2 T nutritional yeast flakes
1 tsp. onion granules
½ tsp. mustard powder
½ tsp. garlic granules

1⅓ C unbleached all-purpose flour
1 C whole wheat pastry flour
⅓ C whole grain yellow cornmeal
2 tsp. non-aluminum baking
    powder
1 tsp. crushed red pepper flakes
¾ tsp. salt
½ tsp. baking soda

2 large scallions, sliced

Preheat the oven to 400°F.

Place the first seven ingredients in a blender, and process until completely smooth.

In a large bowl, stir together the remaining dry ingredients. Make a well in the center, and pour in the blended mixture and scallions. Stir everything together until moistened. Do not over-mix.

Drop by rounded spoonfuls onto an oiled or non-stick baking sheet, and bake for 20-22 minutes or until the bottoms are just barely browned. Cool on wire racks. Serve warm or at room temperature.

Per biscuit: Calories: 107, Protein: 4 gm., Carbohydrates: 22 gm., Fat: 0 gm.

Cheezy Corn Spoon Bread

Yield: serves 4

Spoon bread is a soft, fluffy baked product with a cornmeal base, and is typically used in place of bread, potatoes, or rice. It's baked in a casserole and served, of course, with a spoon. Accompany it with steamed greens, brightly colored vegetables, and perhaps a crunchy salad.

Have ready:

1 C Colby Cheeze, p. 20, shredded

1 C whole grain yellow cornmeal
¾ tsp. salt
3 C water
1 (10.5 oz.) pkg. firm silken tofu, drained and crumbled
2 C frozen corn kernels, thawed* (measure after thawing)
¼ C dried onion flakes
2 T All-Season Blend, p. 93
several drops of Tabasco sauce, to taste

Preheat the oven to 350°F.

In a medium saucepan, mix together the cornmeal, salt, and 1 cup of the water to make a smooth paste. Gradually stir in the remaining water. Bring to a boil, stirring constantly. Cover, reduce the heat to low, and simmer for 15 minutes, stirring occasionally.

Meanwhile, place the tofu in a blender or food processor, and blend until smooth and creamy, stopping occasionally to push the tofu down into the blades with a spatula. Transfer the tofu to a bowl, and stir in the cooked cornmeal and remaining ingredients, including the cheeze. Mix thoroughly.

Spoon the mixture evenly into an oiled or nonstick 8" x 8" baking dish or similarly sized casserole. Bake for 35-40 minutes or until the top is nicely browned. Let stand for 10-15 minutes before serving.

Per serving: Calories: 302, Protein: 13 gm., Carbohydrates: 49 gm., Fat: 6 gm.

Chili Cheeze Spoon Bread

Add 1 (4 oz.) can diced green chili peppers, drained, to the cooked cornmeal mixture.

*Note: To thaw frozen corn, transfer to a mesh strainer and place under hot running tap water, carefully stirring until completely thawed. Drain well.

Quiches, Casseroles & Entrées

Quiche Laverne

Yield: one 10-inch quiche (serves 6)

Quiche Lorraine is a very special, French onion pie, traditionally made with a custard of eggs and cream that is seasoned with onions, Gruyère or Swiss cheese, and bacon. Our delicious, offbeat, Laverne version has a crispy potato crust, is totally vegetarian, much lower in fat, and completely cholesterol-free.

2 C potatoes, shredded
¼ C onion, grated
3 T unbleached all-purpose flour
½ tsp. salt
2 tsp. canola oil

1 head cauliflower, broken into bite-size florets, steamed (about 4½ cups)
1 (10.5 oz.) pkg. firm silken tofu
1¼ C water
⅓ C nutritional yeast flakes
⅓ C quick-cooking rolled oats
4 T arrowroot or cornstarch
3 T fresh lemon juice
1 T onion granules
1 tsp. salt
½ tsp. garlic granules
⅛ tsp. turmeric

½ C scallions, thinly sliced
2 T vegetarian bacon bits (optional)
paprika

Preheat the oven to 400°F. For the crust, place the potatoes and onion in a bowl, and toss together. Sprinkle on the flour and salt, and toss again, using a fork or your hands. Pat into a non-stick or well-oiled 10-inch pie plate, using your fingers to spread the mixture evenly over the bottom and up the sides. Bake for 30 minutes. Remove from the oven and brush the oil over the crust, or spread it evenly using the back of a spoon. Return the crust to the oven to crispen and bake for 15 minutes more, until the surface is lightly browned. Let cool while you prepare the filling. Reduce the oven temperature to 375°F.

Prepare the cauliflower and steam until tender. Refresh under cold water to stop the cooking. Drain and transfer to a large bowl.

Place the next ten ingredients in a blender, and process until the oats are finely ground and the sauce is completely smooth. Pour into a saucepan along with the scallions, and bring to a boil, stirring constantly. Reduce the heat to low and continue to cook, beating constantly with a wire whisk or wooden spoon, until very thick and smooth. Remove from the heat and stir in the

...continued on next page

vegetarian bacon bits, if using. Pour over the cauliflower, mixing well. The sauce will be thick and stretchy.

Spoon the filling into the crust, and dust the top liberally with paprika. Bake for 25-30 minutes, until golden brown. Let rest for 10 minutes. Serve warm or at room temperature. This is also delicious cold the following day.

Per serving: Calories: 184, Protein: 8 gm., Carbohydrates: 28 gm., Fat: 4 gm.

Grated Potato Gratin

Yield: serves 6

This is an interesting and versatile dish—cheezy grated potatoes and onions baked and served in wedges. It may be used as a main dish pie, plain or garnished with applesauce, Tofu Sour Cream, pg. 90, ketchup, or Marinara Sauce, pg. 92. It can also be used as a "crust" and topped with bite-size, assorted steamed vegetables, lightly seasoned with lemon juice or stirred into a rich, non-dairy cream sauce.

1 large red or yellow onion, grated
3 medium potatoes, peeled and
   shredded
4 T nutritional yeast flakes
1 T unbleached all-purpose flour
½ tsp. salt
¼ tsp. dried thyme leaves
pinch of freshly grated nutmeg,
   or ground nutmeg
freshly ground black pepper,
   to taste

Preheat the oven to 400°F.

Place the onion and potatoes in a large bowl, and mix together. Sprinkle the remaining ingredients over the vegetables, and mix thoroughly, using your hands if necessary, to distribute the seasonings evenly.

Spoon the mixture into an oiled or non-stick 10-inch pie plate, spreading and patting it out as evenly as possible over the bottom and up the sides of the pan. Bake for 40-45 minutes, until firm and golden. Serve in wedges, hot or at room temperature.

Per serving: Calories: 88, Protein: 3 gm., Carbohydrates: 18 gm., Fat: 0 gm.

Florentine Ricotta Pie

Yield: one 10-inch pie (8 servings)

A hearty, savory dinner pie that is delicious warm, at room temperature, or even served cold the following day. It makes an elegant entrée for dinner or special luncheons and is surprisingly filling.

Have ready:

1 recipe Flaky Pie Crust, p. 176

2 (10 oz.) pkgs. frozen chopped
   spinach, thawed
1 C scallions, thinly sliced
½ lb. firm regular tofu, drained and
   well mashed
1 tsp. dried basil leaves
½ tsp. dried marjoram leaves

1½ C water
⅓ C quick-cooking rolled oats
¼ C nutritional yeast flakes
4 T tahini
4 T fresh lemon juice
2 T arrowroot or cornstarch
1¼ tsp. salt
1 tsp. onion powder
½ tsp. mustard powder

Preheat the oven to 400°F. Prepare the crust and pre-bake for 10-15 minutes, until lightly golden brown. Let cool. Reduce the oven temperature to 350°F.

Place the spinach in a mesh strainer, and press or squeeze to remove as much moisture as possible. Transfer to a bowl and stir in the scallions, tofu, basil, and marjoram. Mix well and set aside.

Place the remaining ingredients in a blender, and process several minutes until very smooth. Pour over the spinach mixture, and mix thoroughly. Spoon the filling into the cooled crust, and bake for 40-50 minutes, or until the center of the pie is firm and the crust is golden brown. Cool for 15 minutes. Serve warm or at room temperature. This is also delicious cold the following day.

Per serving: Calories: 274, Protein: 10 gm., Carbohydrates: 30 gm., Fat: 12 gm.

Fabuloso Kale Casserole

Yield: 6 servings

Kale is a nutritional powerhouse with a chewy, "meaty" texture. The marriage of kale and creamy, cheddar-flavored rice in this luscious casserole pie makes for a truly satisfying meal. Serve it with beets, bread, and whatever else suits your fancy.

Have ready:

3 C cooked rice (brown, basmati, wild, or a medley of 2 or 3 kinds)
1 recipe Simply Cheezy Sauce, p. 75

5 C kale, chopped, or 2 (10 oz.) pkgs. frozen cut leaf kale
¼ C water
1 T fresh lemon juice
2 cloves garlic, pressed or minced
1 C red onion, sliced
2 C mushrooms, sliced
1 medium carrot, shredded
½ tsp. salt, or to taste
freshly ground black pepper, to taste

Preheat the oven to 350°F. Fold the cheeze sauce into the hot rice, and mix well. Spread the mixture on the bottom of a lightly oiled or non-stick 10-inch glass pie plate or 2-quart casserole dish, and set aside.

Steam the fresh kale or cook the frozen kale according to the package directions. Place the cooked greens in a mesh strainer, and press or squeeze to remove as much moisture as possible. Set aside.

Heat the water and lemon juice in a skillet. Add the garlic, onion, and mushrooms, and cook over medium high, stirring almost constantly, until the vegetables are tender and the liquid has evaporated. Stir in the drained kale and shredded carrot. Season with salt and pepper to taste.

Spoon the vegetables over the rice mixture already in the pie plate or casserole dish. Bake for 25 minutes. Let rest for 10 minutes before serving; serve hot.

Per serving: Calories: 277, Protein: 9 gm., Carbohydrates: 47 gm., Fat: 5 gm.

Tofu Tetrazzini

Yield: 6 servings

Tetrazzini is a main dish casserole that typically includes cooked chicken or turkey, pasta, mushrooms, and almonds in a rich cream sauce topped with Parmesan cheese. With a few adaptations, we've created a fabulous, healthful, totally vegetarian version.

1 lb. spaghetti, broken in half
¼ C water + 1 T balsamic vinegar or
    fresh lemon juice,
    or 4 T non-alcoholic white wine
4 C (about 12 ounces in weight)
    fresh mushrooms, thinly sliced
1 small red, orange, or green bell
    pepper, chopped
1 C unbleached all-purpose flour
4 C low-fat, dairy-free (vegan) milk
3 T All-Season Blend, p. 93
1 T onion granules
1 tsp. garlic granules
½ tsp. salt
1 C frozen green peas, defrosted
½ lb. firm regular tofu, cut in ¼-inch
    cubes

Have ready:

½ C Parmazano, p. 25

Preheat the oven to 350°F.

Cook the spaghetti until al dente. Drain and place in a large mixing bowl.

Meanwhile, heat the water and vinegar or lemon juice (or white wine) in a large saucepan. Add the mushrooms and pepper, and cook until tender.

Place the flour, half of the milk, and all of the seasonings in a blender, and process until smooth. Pour over the mushrooms and pepper along with the remaining milk. Mix well and cook, stirring constantly, until slightly thickened and bubbly. Stir in the peas. Pour over the pasta and toss the pasta with the sauce and cubed tofu.

Turn into an oiled, 10" x 14" four-quart casserole dish. Sprinkle the Parmazano on top. Bake for 30-35 minutes or until heated through and golden brown. Serve at once.

For interesting variations, replace the tofu with 8 oz. cubed tempeh, steamed for 15-20 minutes, or 2 C asparagus, cut diagonally and steamed until crisp-tender.

Per serving: Calories: 359, Protein: 18 gm., Carbohydrates: 60 gm., Fat: 4 gm.

Pasta Primavera

Yield: 6 servings

An outstanding vegetable and pasta combination married with a magnificent béchamel sauce. Garnish with freshly ground pepper, fresh parsley, and Parmazano, *pg. 25.*

3 T water + 1 T fresh lemon juice,
   or 4 T non-alcoholic white wine
1 small onion, sliced
2 cloves garlic, minced
1 head broccoli, thinly sliced
1 red bell pepper, sliced into thin
   strips
12 large, fresh mushrooms, thinly
   sliced
1 C frozen peas, thawed
½ C black olives, sliced
½ C fresh basil leaves, torn and
   lightly packed

2 C low-fat, dairy-free (vegan) milk
1 C water
½ C unbleached all-purpose flour
3 T All-Season Blend, p. 93
2 tsp. onion granules
1 tsp. garlic granules
½ tsp. salt
pinch of ground white pepper

1 lb. fettuccine

Heat the water and lemon juice (or wine) in a large skillet or wok, and cook the onion, garlic, and broccoli pieces for 5 minutes. Add the pepper strips and mushrooms. Cook for 5-10 minutes, or until just crisp-tender. Stir in the thawed peas, and cook for 5 minutes longer. Add the olives and basil. Cover and set aside.

For a cheezy béchamel sauce, place the next eight ingredients in a blender, and process until smooth. Pour into a medium saucepan, and cook over medium, stirring almost constantly, until slightly thickened (about 10-15 minutes). Cover and remove from the heat.

While the sauce is heating, cook the fettuccine in a large pot of boiling water until al dente. Drain; transfer to a large bowl or return to the pot, and toss with the warm sauce and vegetables. Serve immediately.

Per serving: Calories: 263, Protein: 11 gm., Carbohydrates: 47 gm., Fat: 3 gm.

Fettuccine Alfonso

Yield: 6 servings

A power-packed, noble version of the classic Alfredo dish, featuring the venerable ribbon noodle. Serve with a crisp, tossed salad and fresh Italian bread, and your meal is complete.

1½ C frozen corn kernels
1½ C low-fat, non-dairy (vegan) milk
2 T tahini (optional)
1 T onion granules
1 tsp. salt

1 (15.5 oz.) can Great Northern
    beans, rinsed and drained well

1 lb. fettuccine

cracked black pepper

Thaw the corn kernels by transferring them to a mesh strainer and placing them under hot, running tap water. Stir carefully until completely thawed, drain well, and measure.

Place the corn, milk, tahini, if using, and seasonings in a blender, and process until completely smooth. (It may take several minutes of processing to completely pulverize the corn.) Pour the blended mixture in a medium saucepan, and stir in the beans. Warm over medium-low until the beans are heated through, stirring often.

While the sauce is heating, cook the fettuccine in a large pot of boiling water until al dente. Drain well and return to the pot. Add the hot sauce and toss until evenly coated. Serve immediately, topping each portion with a generous amount of cracked pepper.

Per serving: Calories: 251, Protein: 11 gm., Carbohydrates: 50 gm., Fat: 1 gm.

Zucchini Feta Fritters

Yield: 14-16 fritters

These super supper cakes are absolutely scrumptious. Try them garnished with a dollop of Tofu Sour Cream, *pg. 90, and a fresh spearmint leaf or two, if available.*

½ C whole wheat pastry flour
½ C unbleached all-purpose flour
½ tsp. baking powder
½ tsp. baking soda
1 T arrowroot or cornstarch
½ tsp. salt

½ C low-fat, dairy-free (vegan) milk
2 medium zucchini, shredded
¼ C scallions, thinly sliced
1½ tsp. dried spearmint leaves,
    or 1 T minced fresh spearmint
    leaves
freshly ground black pepper, to
    taste

Have ready:
1 heaping C Betta Feta, p. 28,
    drained and crumbled

Place the flours, baking powder, baking soda, arrowroot or cornstarch, and salt in a large mixing bowl, and stir with a wire whisk to combine well.

In a separate bowl, place the milk, shredded zucchini, scallions, spearmint, pepper, and Betta Feta, and mix well. Stir the wet ingredients into the flour mixture, and mix until everything is thoroughly combined.

Lightly oil a large griddle or skillet (or use a non-stick pan), and heat over medium-high. When the griddle is very hot (water dropped on it beads and dances across the surface), spoon or pour on the batter, using a scant ¼ cup for each cake. Carefully turn the fritters over when their bottoms are a deep golden brown. Cook the second side briefly, just until well browned. Add a few drops of oil to the pan between cooking each batch, if necessary. Keep warm in a 250°F oven while the remainder cook. Serve warm garnished with *Tofu Sour Cream*, pg. 90.

Per fritter: Calories: 55, Protein: 3 gm., Carbohydrates: 8 gm., Fat: 1 gm.

Macaroni & Tomatoes

Yield: 8 servings

This stovetop casserole was a staple in my husband's family, where it was traditionally prepared with lots of butter and processed cheese. With a few adaptations, the butter and cheese were removed, while the flavor and consistency were enhanced. This is a hearty and filling entrée and is especially appealing to children.

2 large onions, finely chopped
½ C water + 2 T balsamic vinegar
    or fresh lemon juice, or ½ C
    non-alcoholic white wine
¼ tsp. turmeric
1 lb. elbow macaroni
½ C water
½ C unsalted tomato juice
⅓ C raw cashew pieces
1 T tahini
2 T fresh lemon juice
2 T quick-cooking rolled oats
¼ C nutritional yeast flakes
1¼ tsp. salt
1 tsp. onion granules
½ tsp. garlic powder
½ tsp. mustard powder
2 (16 oz.) cans unsalted whole
    tomatoes, including juice (about
    4 cups)
freshly ground black pepper, to
    taste

Combine the onions, water, and vinegar or lemon juice (or wine) in a large pot, cover, and braise for 15 minutes. Stir in the turmeric, and continue cooking, uncovered, until the onions are soft and the liquid has evaporated (about 10 minutes.)

While the onions are cooking, boil the macaroni in a large pot of water until al dente. Drain and set aside.

Place the water, tomato juice, cashews, tahini, lemon juice, rolled oats, yeast flakes, and seasonings in a blender, and process until completely smooth. Set aside.

When the onions are finished cooking, stir in the cooked macaroni. Add the canned tomatoes and their juice, carefully breaking the tomatoes apart with your mixing spoon. Then add the blended mixture and plenty of freshly ground black pepper, stirring well to thoroughly combine. Cook over medium, stirring often, for about 8-12 minutes until hot and bubbly.

Per serving: Calories: 168, Protein: 6 gm., Carbohydrates: 27 gm., Fat: 4 gm.

Baked Macaroni & Cheeze

Yield: 8 servings

This version of the popular American standard is just as spectacular as its dairy counterpart—possibly even better, since it has no cholesterol! This recipe is reminiscent of "cafeteria style" macaroni and cheese—it has a dry rather than creamy consistency, because as it bakes, the "cheese" forms tiny curds around the pasta. Kids of all ages will adore it.

¼ C water + 1 T balsamic vinegar
    or fresh lemon juice
1 large onion, finely chopped
1 lb. elbow macaroni or ziti
2 C water
½ C pimiento pieces, drained
½ C raw cashew pieces
⅓ C fresh lemon juice
⅓ C nutritional yeast flakes
4 T non-alcoholic white wine
    or mirin
2 tsp. onion granules
2 tsp. garlic granules
1 tsp. salt

Preheat the oven to 350°F.

Heat the water and vinegar or lemon juice in a large saucepan. Add the onion, cover, and cook, stirring occasionally, until tender and lightly browned (about 15-20 minutes). If the onion sticks to the pan, add a few teaspoons more water to help loosen it.

Meanwhile, cook the macaroni in boiling water until al dente. Drain and stir into the cooked onions. Mix well.

Process the remaining ingredients in a blender for several minutes until completely smooth. Stir the blended mixture into the macaroni and onions, and spoon into a lightly oiled or non-stick, 3-quart casserole dish. Bake uncovered for 25-35 minutes. Serve immediately.

Per serving: Calories: 149, Protein: 5 gm., Carbohydrates: 22 gm., Fat: 5 gm.

Noodles Ramona

Yield: 6 servings

Our spin-off of the ever-popular "Noodles Romanoff" is an effortless, cheeseless rendering of this esteemed "pasta and cheddar" delight.

1 (15.5 oz.) can white beans, rinsed
 well and drained (about 1½ C)
1 C low-fat, dairy-free (vegan) milk
½ C pimiento pieces, drained
6 T nutritional yeast flakes
2 T tahini (optional)
3 T fresh lemon juice
½ tsp. salt

1 lb. thin fettuccine, broken in half
 or thirds
4 T fresh parsley, chopped

Purée the first seven ingredients in a blender until completely smooth. Transfer to a medium saucepan, and warm gently over low, stirring constantly and taking care not to boil.

Meanwhile, cook the fettuccine in boiling water until al dente. Drain and return to the pot, or transfer to a large mixing bowl. Toss with the warm sauce. Garnish each serving with parsley.

Per serving: Calories: 218, Protein: 11 gm., Carbohydrates: 41 gm., Fat: 0 gm.

Cheeze, Bread & Tomato Soufflé

Yield: 6 servings

A simple casserole for busy nights or whenever fresh tomatoes are abundant.

1½ C water
½ C pimiento pieces, drained
½ C raw cashew pieces
3 T nutritional yeast flakes
3 T fresh lemon juice
2 T non-alcoholic white wine
    (optional)
1½ tsp. onion granules
1¼ tsp. salt
½ tsp. mustard powder
½ tsp. dried thyme leaves
½ tsp. garlic granules
lots of freshly ground black pepper,
    to taste

6-9 thick slices whole grain bread
    (crusts may be removed, if
    desired)
3 fresh, ripe tomatoes, sliced

Place all the ingredients except the bread and tomatoes in a blender, and process several minutes until completely smooth. Set aside.

Preheat the oven to 375°F.

Oil a 2-quart baking dish or soufflé dish. Place a layer of 2-3 slices of bread in the bottom of the dish followed by a layer of the tomatoes and ⅓ of the blended sauce, then another layer of bread and tomatoes followed by another ⅓ of the sauce. Finish with a final layer of bread and tomatoes followed by the remainder of the sauce. Bake for 45-50 minutes, or until lightly puffed and golden brown. Serve immediately.

Per serving: Calories: 199, Protein: 8 gm., Carbohydrates: 26 gm., Fat: 7 gm.

Spinach and Cheeze Soufflé

Prepare *Cheeze, Bread & Tomato Soufflé*, replacing the tomatoes with 1 (10 oz.) pkg. frozen chopped spinach, cooked according to the package directions. Drain well in a wire mesh strainer, pressing firmly with the back of a spoon to express as much liquid as possible. Place in a blender with the remaining ingredients except the bread. Include the non-alcoholic white wine, increasing the amount to ¼ cup. Process into a very smooth pureé; this will take several minutes. Layer the bread and sauce, and continue the recipe directions.

Mushroom and Cheeze Soufflé

Prepare *Cheeze, Bread & Tomato Soufflé*, replacing the tomatoes with 1 lb. of fresh mushrooms, thinly sliced and cooked in 3 T non-alcoholic white wine until tender and the liquid has evaporated. Set aside. Blend the ingredients as for *Cheeze, Bread & Tomato Soufflé*, increasing the non-alcoholic white wine to ¼ cup. Layer the bread, mushrooms, and sauce, and continue the recipe directions.

Corn and Cheeze Soufflé

Prepare *Cheeze, Bread & Tomato Soufflé*, replacing the tomatoes with 1½ C frozen corn kernels, thawed under hot running tap water in a wire mesh strainer. Drain and set aside. Blend the ingredients as for *Cheeze, Bread & Tomato Soufflé*, increasing the non-alcoholic white wine to ¼ cup. Layer the bread, corn, and sauce, and continue the recipe directions. Alternately, the corn may be pureéd with the sauce ingredients.

Golden Pasta & Cauliflower Salad

Yield: 8 servings

An unusual but elegant salad that is equally delicious and creamy served warm or chilled. This is a hearty cool weather entrée as well as a welcome addition to hot weather picnics and year-round pot luck suppers.

1 large head cauliflower, broken
    into small florets
1 lb. radiatore,
    or other small pasta
1 C scallions, thinly sliced
½ C smooth or crunchy natural,
    unsweetened peanut butter
¼ C tamari
2 tsp. toasted sesame oil
¼ C brown rice vinegar
¼ C nutritional yeast flakes
2 T fresh lemon juice
1¼ C water
several drops Tabasco sauce, to
    taste
1 large red bell pepper, finely
    chopped
1 (8 oz.) can sliced water chestnuts,
    rinsed and drained

Bring a large pot of water to a boil. Add the cauliflower and stir. When the water returns to a boil, add the pasta and cook the cauliflower and pasta together until the pasta is al dente. Drain well and place in a very large mixing bowl. Stir in the scallions and let them lightly steam with the hot pasta while you prepare the sauce.

Cream together the peanut butter, tamari, toasted sesame oil, brown rice vinegar, nutritional yeast flakes, and lemon juice. Gradually add the water, beating in a small amount at a time. When smooth, add the hot pepper sauce to taste.

Stir the sauce, bell pepper, and water chestnuts into the pasta, and toss gently but thoroughly until the sauce is evenly distributed. Serve warm, chilled, or at room temperature.

Per serving: Calories: 217, Protein: 8 gm., Carbohydrates: 25 gm., Fat: 9 gm.

Stuffed Baked Potatoes

Yield: 6 servings

Stuffed potatoes are most frequently served in restaurants where they are savored as a gourmet treat. They are also usually loaded with a lot of high-fat, high-salt ingredients such as butter, cream, cheese, bacon, etc. But preparing delicious, low-fat stuffed potatoes at home is actually very easy to do. The following recipe eliminates the pitfalls of standard stuffed potatoes while capturing all that is best loved about them—the creamy texture and unbeatable, savory flavor. Although traditionally served as a side dish, stuffed potatoes are quite hearty as a main dish when served with one or two steamed vegetables and a salad.

6 large baking potatoes (about 3½ lbs.)
1 tsp. salt
freshly ground black pepper, to taste
½ C nutritional yeast flakes
¼ tsp. Tabasco sauce, more or less to taste (optional)
1¼ C low-fat, dairy-free (vegan) milk, as needed
2 T vegetarian bacon bits
1 C scallions, thinly sliced
paprika

Scrub the potatoes and pat them dry. Prick them all over with a fork, and bake directly on the center oven rack in a preheated 400°F oven for 1 to 1½ hours, or until very tender. Remove them from the oven using an oven mitt, and slice each potato in half lengthwise. Scoop out the pulp with a spoon, leaving about ¼ inch of potato pulp in each shell to help it keep its shape. Place the pulp in a large mixing bowl. Place the scooped out shells on a large, ungreased cookie sheet, and set aside.

Using a hand masher or electric beater, mash or whip the potatoes until they are smooth. (Do not use a food processor as this will make the potatoes gluey.) Beat in the salt, pepper, nutritional yeast, and Tabasco sauce. Gradually beat in the milk, using just enough to make the potatoes creamy and soft but not runny. Stir in the vegetarian bacon bits and scallions, and mix until evenly distributed.

...continued on next page

Spoon the potato mixture into the reserved shells, distributing it among them as uniformly as possible. Sprinkle the tops of the potatoes with paprika, and return them to the 400°F oven to bake for 20-25 minutes, or until lightly browned on top. Serve hot.

Per serving: Calories: 209, Protein: 7 gm., Carbohydrates: 44 gm., Fat: 0 gm.

Note: Stuffed potatoes may be prepared in advance and stored several hours or overnight in the refrigerator, loosely covered with foil, plastic wrap, or waxed paper. If chilled, add an additional 5 minutes to the final baking time.

Stovetop Cheezy Rotini

Yield: 6 servings

Corkscrew pasta in a thick, cheezy sauce, complemented by red bell pepper and toasted walnuts. This is a busy day favorite—it can be whipped up in under 15 minutes! Garnish with cracked black pepper and a little chopped, fresh basil, if you have it on hand.

Have ready:

1 recipe Simply Cheezy Sauce (using 1½ tsp. dried basil leaves), p. 75

1 lb. rotini (corkscrew) pasta

1 small red bell pepper, minced
¼ C walnuts, toasted and chopped

Prepare the Simply Cheezy Sauce, cover, and keep warm. Cook the rotini until al dente. Drain well and return it to the pot. Stir the sauce, red bell pepper, and walnuts into the pasta, mixing well. Serve at once.

Per serving: Calories: 232, Protein: 8 gm., Carbohydrates: 31 gm., Fat: 8 gm.

Mediterranean Pasta

Yield: 6 servings

A delectable blend of garlic, tomatoes, and the flavor of feta cheese. Serve with a leafy green salad and perhaps some thinly sliced radishes and cucumbers.

1 lb. spaghetti

3 T water + 1 T fresh lemon juice,
   or 4 T non-alcoholic white wine
3-5 cloves garlic, minced
3 fresh, ripe tomatoes, coarsely
   chopped

½ C black olives, sliced
2 C Betta Feta, p. 28, well crumbled,
   with its marinade
freshly ground black pepper,
   to taste

Cook the spaghetti until al dente. Drain and set aside.

While the pasta is cooking, heat the water and lemon juice (or wine) in a small skillet; add the garlic, and cook for 2 minutes. Add the chopped tomatoes and cook until just slightly softened.

Return the pasta to the cooking pot, or transfer it to a large bowl. Toss with the seasoned cooking liquid and tomatoes, olives, Betta Feta and marinade, and lots of freshly ground black pepper. Serve immediately.

Per serving: Calories: 246, Protein: 12 gm., Carbohydrates: 31 gm., Fat: 7 gm.

Garbanzos With Spinach & Betta Feta

Yield: 4½ cups (4 servings)

A Mediterranean-inspired medley that is superb over couscous, rice, millet, or cracked wheat. Serve with plenty of extra lemon wedges on the side.

Have ready:

1 recipe Betta Feta, p. 28, drained and crumbled (set marinade aside for use in mixture below)

1 (15 oz.) can garbanzo beans (about 1½ C), rinsed well and drained

2 (10 oz.) pkgs. frozen chopped spinach, cooked and drained well

marinade from Betta Feta (see above)

1 tsp. ground cumin

3 T fresh lemon juice
lots of freshly ground black pepper, to taste

Place the beans, spinach, marinade, and cumin in a large saucepan, and cook, stirring often, until hot (about 10 minutes).

Stir in the lemon juice and crumbled Betta Feta, and season with pepper. Serve warm or at room temperature.

Per serving: Calories: 367, Protein: 21 gm., Carbohydrates: 44 gm., Fat: 10 gm.

Potatoes Gruyère

Yield: 6-8 servings

A hearty au gratin potato casserole. Serve with a steamed vegetable, salad, and crusty rolls.

1¼ C water
1 C firm silken tofu, drained and
    crumbled
½ C raw cashew pieces
¼ C nutritional yeast flakes
2 T fresh lemon juice
1 T onion granules
½ tsp. garlic granules
⅛ tsp. freshly grated nutmeg,
    or ground nutmeg

1 small onion, finely chopped
½ C scallions, sliced

6 medium white potatoes, peeled
    and thinly sliced
salt and freshly ground black
    pepper, to taste

To make a Gruyère sauce, place the first eight ingredients in a blender, and process several minutes until the mixture is completely smooth. Then stir in the onion and scallions.

Preheat the oven to 350°F.

Oil a large, deep casserole dish, arrange in it a layer of the potatoes, and sprinkle with salt and a generous amount of black pepper. Drizzle on some of the blended sauce, then more of the potatoes, salt and pepper, more of the sauce, and so on, finishing with a layer of sauce. Cover and bake for one hour; then uncover and bake about 45 minutes more, until the potatoes are very tender, and the top is golden brown. Let rest 10 minutes before serving. Serve hot.

Per serving: Calories: 109, Protein: 7 gm., Carbohydrates: 31 gm., Fat: 6 gm.

Frittata

Yield: 6 servings

Somewhere between a baked Western cheese omelet and an Italian-style, crustless quiche, this delicious, egg-free frittata is creamy, "custardy," and chock full of potatoes, onions, and peppers. Scoop it onto warm plates, and serve with toast for a soothing breakfast, brunch, or light supper.

¼ C water
2 cloves garlic, pressed
1 medium onion, chopped
1 large potato, peeled and diced
1 large green bell pepper, cut into
    small dice

1 lb. firm regular tofu, drained,
    patted dry, and crumbled
1 (16 oz.) can unsalted, whole
    tomatoes, with juice
⅓ C unbleached all-purpose flour
1 T cornstarch
1 T nutritional yeast flakes
1 tsp. salt
½ tsp. dried oregano leaves
¼ tsp. turmeric
⅛ tsp. freshly ground black pepper

In a medium skillet, heat the water and add the garlic, onion, potato, and green pepper. Cover and cook, stirring occasionally, until the potato is tender (about 10 minutes).

Preheat the oven to 350°F.

While the vegetables are cooking, place the remaining ingredients in a blender, and process until velvety smooth. Transfer to a bowl. Stir in the cooked vegetables, and mix well. Pour evenly into two oiled or non-stick, 10-inch pie pans, and bake for 45-50 minutes. Let rest for 10-15 minutes before serving.

Per serving: Calories: 139, Protein: 8 gm., Carbohydrates: 18 gm., Fat: 4 gm.

Cauliflower Benedict

Yield: 8 servings

This recipe, a spin-off of the classic Eggs Benedict, is made with cauliflower instead of eggs, marinated seitan instead of Canadian bacon, and a cheezy, eggless, hollandaise-style sauce. Try it with steamed asparagus spears served on the side.

¼ C apple cider vinegar
½ C water
1 T tamari
1 tsp. toasted sesame oil
1 tsp. garlic granules
1 tsp. ground ginger
1 lb. seitan, drained well and thinly sliced

1 medium cauliflower, broken into 8 large florets

Have ready:
1 recipe Simply Cheezy Sauce, p. 75

4 whole grain English muffins, split and toasted
paprika

To make *Marinated Seitan*, whisk together the vinegar, water, tamari, sesame oil, garlic granules, and ginger. Pour into a non-metal bowl, and add the seitan slices, turning several times to coat well. Cover and let soak in the refrigerator for 30 minutes or longer, turning the seitan occasionally to make sure that all the pieces remain coated.

Steam the cauliflower until crisp-tender. Drain, set aside, and keep warm.

Prepare the Simply Cheezy Sauce as directed. Cover and keep warm.

To assemble, drain the seitan slices and distribute them evenly over the toasted English muffin halves. Top each muffin half with a cauliflower floret, then cover with the hot Simply Cheezy Sauce. Garnish with the paprika and serve immediately (with a knife and fork).

Per serving: Calories: 256, Protein: 25 gm., Carbohydrates: 27 gm., Fat: 5 gm.

Green Bean Stovetop Casserole

Yield: 6 servings

When I was growing up, my sister Peggy's favorite "vegetable" was green bean casserole. Although she has expanded her repertoire quite a bit since then, this is still a big hit with her and her children. It's soothing, satisfying, and very easy to make.

Have ready:

1 recipe Unprocessed Cheeze
    Sauce, p. 74
3 C hot, cooked rice (brown,
    basmati, or wild rice)

1½ C water
5 C fresh green beans, sliced,
    or frozen cut green beans,
    defrosted*
2 C fresh mushrooms, sliced
1 (8 oz.) can water chestnuts,
    drained and diced
salt and freshly ground black
    pepper, to taste

paprika

Prepare the sauce as directed, cover, and keep warm.

Place the water in a large saucepan, and bring to a boil. Add the green beans and mushrooms. Cover and reduce the heat to medium. Cook until the green beans are tender, about 5 minutes. Drain well. Return the vegetables to the saucepan, and stir in the warm sauce, hot rice, and diced water chestnuts. Mix well. Season with salt and pepper.

Serve immediately, garnished generously with paprika.

Per serving: Calories: 260, Protein: 11 gm., Carbohydrates: 47 gm., Fat: 2 gm.

*For variety, try using 5 C broccoli or cauliflower florets, or sliced asparagus instead of green beans.

Tofu Devonshires

Yield: 8 servings

Devonshire sandwiches typically consist of turkey, chicken or seafood, bacon strips, tomato, and a rich, cheddar cheese sauce. In this luscious, vegetarian rendition, tofu replaces the meat, marinated seitan supplants the bacon, and then everything is smothered in a sensuous, non-dairy cheeze sauce. This is a very special lunch, brunch, or light supper meal.

3 C water
3 T All-Season Blend, p. 93
1 lb. firm regular tofu, cut into 8
    equal slabs

In a large saucepan, stir together the water and seasoning. Add the tofu slabs and bring to a boil. Reduce the heat to medium and simmer, uncovered, for 20 minutes, carefully turning the slabs occasionally to make sure that each piece is covered with the liquid. Drain, taking care not to break the slabs, and set aside.

Have ready:

8 slices whole grain bread, toasted
1 recipe Marinated Seitan from
    Cauliflower Benedict, p. 138,
    drained
2 fresh, ripe tomatoes, sliced
1 recipe Mornay Sauce, p. 85

Preheat the oven to 400°F.

Place the toast on a dry or lightly oiled baking sheet. Distribute the seitan slices evenly over all. Top with the tofu slabs and tomato slices. Spoon the Mornay Sauce evenly over each Devonshire. Bake for 15 minutes, until bubbly and the tops are golden brown. Using a spatula, carefully transfer the Devonshires to warm plates, and serve immediately (with a knife and fork).

Per serving: Calories: 317, Protein: 31 gm., Carbohydrates: 27 gm., Fat: 9 gm.

Spinach Ricotta Balls

Yield: 32 balls (8 servings)

These firm, tasty balls are amazingly versatile. They are delicious plain, with ketchup, or with your favorite tomato sauce. Try them on top of spaghetti and begin a new tradition. They are even great cold as a snack, or for lunch the following day on bread with a little ketchup or dairy-free mayonnaise.

Have ready:

1 (10 oz.) pkg. frozen, chopped
    spinach
⅔ C Parmazano, p. 25

1 lb. firm regular tofu, drained and
    well mashed
¾ C dairy-free (vegan) mayonnaise
½ C whole grain yellow cornmeal
⅓ C unbleached all-purpose flour,
    or whole wheat pastry flour
2 tsp. garlic granules
1 tsp. onion granules
½ tsp. salt
¼ tsp. ground dill seed,
    or ground caraway seed
lots of freshly ground black pepper,
    to taste

Cook the spinach according to the package directions. Place in a wire mesh strainer to drain. Press firmly to express all the liquid, and set aside.

Preheat the oven to 350°F.

To make a ricotta mixture, place the remaining ingredients in a bowl, and mix thoroughly into a thick paste. Add the cooked spinach and Parmazano, and mix well until evenly distributed. The mixture will be stiff. Form into balls using 2 level tablespoons of the mixture for each, and place on an oiled or non-stick baking sheet. Bake for 35-40 minutes until firm and lightly browned.

Per serving: Calories: 201, Protein: 10 gm., Carbohydrates: 18 gm., Fat: 8 gm.

Spinafel Sandwiches

Yield: about 16 pita halves (16 servings)

A new variation on falafel sandwiches, these stuffed pita pockets are extra light, because they are made with Spinach Ricotta Balls *which are baked, not fried. You can make them with balls that are hot right out of the oven, with reheated balls, or with leftover balls straight from the refrigerator. Drizzle them with your favorite fat-free Italian dressing or with our* Orange-Sesame Vinaigrette *for a tempting contrast in flavors.*

Have ready:

1 recipe (32) Spinach Ricotta Balls, p. 141
8 pita breads, sliced in half to form 2 pockets from each bread

fresh, ripe tomatoes, chopped
iceberg, leaf, and/or romaine lettuce, shredded
black olives, sliced (optional)
cucumber, diced (optional)
mild onion, minced (optional)
grated carrot (optional)

Prepare the Spinach Ricotta Balls according to the directions. Stuff 2 balls into each pita pocket, surrounding them with some of the listed salad garnishes (quantities are up to you). Drizzle with the *Orange-Sesame Vinaigrette*, below, or your favorite fat-free Italian dressing. Serve immediately.

Orange-Sesame Vinaigrette

1 C fresh, unsweetened orange juice
2 T tahini
2 T balsamic vinegar
1 T Dijon mustard
1 small piece of sweet onion

Place all the ingredients in a blender, and process until creamy and smooth. Store in the refrigerator.

Per serving (without vinaigrette): Calories: 180, Protein: 8 gm., Carbohydrates: 25 gm., Fat: 5 gm.

Per serving (with vinaigrette): Calories: 200, Protein: 8 gm., Carbohydrates: 26 gm., Fat: 6 gm.

Three-Cheeze Lasagne

Yield: 10 servings

This is a good dish to prepare when you have a bit of extra time, because it has so many steps. But if the Marinara Sauce, Tofu Ricotta, and Parmazano are made a day or so ahead of time, the final assembly can actually be quite speedy.

Have ready:

1 recipe Marinara Sauce, p. 92,
    or 6 C of your favorite fat-free
    tomato sauce
½ C Parmazano, p. 25
1 recipe Tofu Ricotta, p. 27

1 C water
¼ C fresh lemon juice
¼ C nutritional yeast flakes
3 T tahini
3 T quick-cooking rolled oats
2 T arrowroot or cornstarch
2 tsp. onion granules
½ tsp. salt

15 lasagne noodles

To make a mozzarella cheeze sauce, place the next eight ingredients in a blender, and process until the oats are finely ground and the sauce is completely smooth. Set aside.

Cook the lasagne noodles in boiling water for 7-9 minutes or until just barely done. Drain, rinse with cold water, and drain again.

Preheat the oven to 350°F.

Place 1 cup of Marinara Sauce over the bottom of an oiled 9" x 13" pan. Layer in ⅓ of the lasagne noodles, slightly overlapping them. Spread with ½ of the Tofu Ricotta. Drizzle on ⅓ of the mozzarella cheeze sauce. Then layer on the next ⅓ of the noodles. Top with half of the remaining Marinara Sauce. Layer on the remaining half of the Tofu Ricotta and another ⅓ of the mozzarella cheeze sauce. Top with the remaining noodles and the rest of the Marinara Sauce. Drizzle the top with the remaining mozzarella cheeze sauce, and sprinkle with the Parmazano.

Bake for 45 minutes. (If some of the ingredients have been prepared ahead of time and are cold, add 5-10 minutes to the baking time.) Let stand for 10 minutes before serving.

Per serving: Calories: 341, Protein: 17 gm., Carbohydrates: 48 gm., Fat: 8 gm.

Luna Melt

Yield: 4 servings

A hot, open-faced sandwich which is simple to put together if you have canned garbanzo beans, egg-free mayonnaise, and Swizz, Mostarella, or Colby Cheeze, on hand.

1½ C cooked garbanzo beans (if
    using canned, rinse well)
¼ C celery, finely chopped
¼ C onion, finely chopped
3 T egg-free (vegan) mayonnaise
1 T fresh lemon juice
½ tsp. All-Season Blend, p. 93
½ tsp. onion granules
¼ tsp. garlic granules
¼ tsp. paprika

4 slices whole grain bread, toasted
1 fresh, ripe tomato, thinly sliced

Have ready:
8 thin slices Swizz, p. 21, Mostarella,
    p. 22, or Colby Cheeze, p. 20

Mash the beans and stir in the next eight ingredients, mixing thoroughly.

Place the toast on a dry baking sheet, and cover each slice with some of the blended spread, distributing it evenly and covering the bread completely to the edges. Top the spread with the tomato slices, and cover each sandwich with 2 slices of cheeze. Broil until the cheeze is lightly browned. Serve immediately.

Per serving: Calories: 288, Protein: 10 gm., Carbohydrates: 38 gm., Fat: 9 gm.

Vegetables Camembert

Yield: 4 servings

A delectable, chunky vegetable sauce with a melty cheeze base. A natural with rice, but equally stupendous on pasta or steamed potatoes.

1 (10.5 oz.) pkg. firm silken tofu,
    drained and crumbled
3 T fresh lemon juice
3 T Dijon mustard
2 T brown rice syrup
½ tsp. salt

1 C frozen peas
¼ C water + 1 T fresh lemon juice
    or balsamic vinegar,
    or 4 T non-alcoholic white wine
1 small onion, thinly sliced
4 cloves garlic, minced
2 red bell peppers, thinly sliced
    lengthwise
2 medium zucchini or yellow
    summer squash, thinly sliced
    on the diagonal
2 scallions, sliced
1 T mirin or non-alcoholic white
    wine
freshly ground black pepper

To make a Camembert sauce, place the first five ingredients in a blender or food processor, and process until smooth and creamy. Set aside.

Thaw the frozen peas by placing them in a colander under hot running tap water. Drain and set aside. In a large wok or saucepan, heat the water and lemon juice or vinegar (or wine), and cook the onion and garlic for 5 minutes. Stir in the peppers and zucchini, and cook for 5 minutes longer. Stir in the peas and scallions, cover, and cook for 1 minute only.

Stir in the Camembert sauce and mirin. Heat, uncovered, over medium-low until warmed through, stirring often. Garnish each serving with freshly ground black pepper.

Per serving: Calories: 138, Protein: 3 gm., Carbohydrates: 25 gm., Fat: 3 gm.

Mattar Paneer

Yield: about 6 cups (6 servings)

The traditional Indian version of this spiced, green pea dish is prepared with a homemade cheese called paneer. *Seasoned tofu easily becomes a convenient and tasty replacement for paneer in this hearty, non-dairy version. Serve with generous portions of basmati rice and warm, fresh chapatis.*

1 lb. firm regular tofu, drained, patted dry, and cut into ½-inch cubes
2 C water
2 T All-Season Blend, p. 93

½ C water + 2 T fresh lemon juice
2 medium onions, halved and thinly sliced
1 T fresh gingerroot, finely chopped, or 4½ tsp. ground ginger
3 cloves garlic, chopped

2 tsp. ground cumin
2 tsp. ground coriander
1 tsp. turmeric
½ tsp. ground cinnamon
¼ tsp. ground nutmeg
¼ tsp. ground black pepper
⅛ tsp. ground cloves
⅛ tsp. cayenne powder, or to taste

Place the tofu cubes, water, and All-Season Blend in a saucepan. Bring to a boil, reduce the heat to medium, and simmer uncovered for 20 minutes, stirring occasionally. Drain and set aside. (The tofu may be prepared ahead of time and refrigerated until needed.)

Heat the water and lemon juice in a large skillet or wok, and cook the onions, covered, until tender (about 10-20 minutes). Add the fresh ginger and garlic, and cook, uncovered, for 2 more minutes. Add the spices and ground ginger, if using, and stir-fry for 2 minutes. Place in a blender along with the ½ cup of water and ½ cup of juice from the tomatoes. Process until smooth.

Pour the blended mixture back into the skillet. Add the tomatoes and the remaining juice, breaking the tomatoes apart with a fork or the side of a spoon. Simmer uncovered over medium for 10 minutes, stirring often. Add the peas, dried cilantro, if using, and reserved tofu. Cover and cook for 10 minutes longer, stirring often, until the peas are

...continued on next page

½ C water
2 C unsalted, canned tomatoes,
    including their juice
4 C frozen peas, thawed under hot
    tap water and drained
¼ C fresh cilantro, chopped,
    or 2 T dried cilantro,
    or 1 T fresh lemon juice

tender and the tofu is hot. Stir in the lemon juice a few minutes before serving, if using. Garnish with the fresh cilantro, if desired.

Per serving: Calories: 191, Protein: 13 gm.,
Carbohydrates: 26 gm., Fat: 4 gm.

Eggplant Newburg

Yield: 6½ cups (4-6 servings)

This is an exciting yet easy way to serve eggplant. It is a perfect topping for grain and pasta, or serve it over split biscuits with a crispy salad on the side. Garnish with cracked black pepper and fresh parsley.

1 medium eggplant, peeled and cut
    into ½-inch dice
12 medium mushrooms, quartered
2 (16 oz.) cans unsalted tomatoes,
    including juice, coarsely
    chopped

½ C mirin, sherry, or non-alcoholic
    red or white wine
¼ C nutritional yeast flakes
¼ C tahini
3 T tamari

Place the eggplant, mushrooms, tomatoes, and their juice in a large skillet or wok, and bring to a boil. Reduce the heat to medium, cover, and simmer, stirring often, until the eggplant is tender but still firm (about 25-30 minutes).

Stir together the remaining ingredients until smooth. Turn off the heat and stir the tahini mixture into the eggplant and tomatoes. Mix until well combined. Serve immediately.

Per serving: Calories: 173, Protein: 8 gm.,
Carbohydrates: 22 gm., Fat: 5 gm.

Eggplant Ricotta

Yield: 6½ cups (6 servings)

Chunks of eggplant and tomato in a seasoned, ricotta-style base. Serve over pasta, polenta or rice, or in a bowl with slices of fresh Italian bread on the side. Especially good over fine Italian capellini.

Have ready:

½ recipe Tofu Cottage Cheeze, p. 27

1 medium eggplant
½ C water + 2 T fresh lemon juice, or ½ C non-alcoholic white wine
2 cloves garlic, finely chopped

2 red or green bell peppers (or 1 of each), cut into strips
½ tsp. salt
lots of freshly ground black pepper, to taste

2 (16 oz.) cans unsalted tomatoes, with juice
1 ½ tsp. dried oregano leaves

Cut the unpeeled eggplant into ½-inch cubes. In a large saucepan or Dutch oven, heat the lemon juice and water (or wine), and add the eggplant and garlic. Cook, uncovered, over medium for 10 minutes, stirring often. Stir in the green pepper strips, salt, and pepper, and cook, uncovered, for 5 minutes longer.

Stir in the tomatoes and oregano, breaking the tomatoes apart with your hands or a fork. Cover and simmer over low, stirring occasionally for 5 minutes more, or until the eggplant is tender.

About 5 minutes before serving, stir the Tofu Cottage Cheeze into the sauce. Cover and continue to cook over low, stirring often, until heated through.

Per serving: Calories: 122, Protein: 5 gm., Carbohydrates: 14 gm., Fat: 4 gm.

Baked Eggplant Parmesan

Yield: 4 servings

In this recipe, the eggplant is broiled instead of breaded and deep fried. Then it is topped with fresh tomato slices and a creamy, mozzarella-style cheeze sauce.

½ C water
3 T nutritional yeast flakes
2 T fresh lemon juice
2 T tahini
2 T quick-cooking rolled oats
1 T arrowroot or cornstarch
1 tsp. onion granules
¼ tsp. salt

1 medium eggplant, unpeeled and
    sliced into ½-inch rounds
2 fresh, ripe tomatoes, thinly sliced

   Have ready:
½ C Parmazano, p. 25

To make the cheeze topping, place the first eight ingredients in a blender, and process until the oats are finely ground and the sauce is completely smooth. Set aside.

Place the eggplant slices on a dry baking sheet. Broil under a preheated broiler about 5 inches from the heat source for about 5 minutes. Turn the slices over with a spatula, and continue broiling until fork tender, only about 2 minutes longer. Remove the eggplant and transfer to a lightly oiled or non-stick baking dish.

Top the eggplant with the tomato slices. Cover with the cheeze topping and sprinkle with the Parmazano. Bake on the center oven rack at 400°F until golden brown and bubbly, about 20-25 minutes.

Per serving: Calories: 224, Protein: 10 gm., Carbohydrates: 24 gm., Fat: 6 gm.

Stuffed Shells

Yield: 16 stuffed shells (serves 8)

Pasta shells brimming with non-dairy ricotta, smothered in a savory marinara sauce, and topped with Parmazano *cheeze.*

Have ready:

16 jumbo pasta stuffing shells, cooked al dente and drained well

1 recipe Marinara Sauce, p. 92, or 6 C of your favorite fat-free tomato sauce

½ C Parmazano, p. 25

1 lb. firm regular tofu, drained and well mashed

⅔ C egg-free (vegan) mayonnaise

1½ T fresh parsley, minced, or 2 tsp. dried parsley flakes

2 tsp. dried basil leaves

2 tsp. onion granules

1 tsp. garlic granules

½ tsp. salt, or to taste

Preheat the oven to 350°F.

In a mixing bowl, combine the tofu, mayonnaise, herbs, and seasonings for the filling, and mash them into a finely grained paste. Stuff about 2 rounded tablespoonfuls of filling into each shell.

Spread a cup or so of Marinara Sauce over the bottom of a 9" x 13" x 2" baking dish. Arrange the stuffed shells in a single layer over the sauce. Spoon the remaining sauce over the shells, and sprinkle with the Parmazano. Bake for 30-45 minutes or until heated through.

Per serving: Calories: 391, Protein: 17 gm., Carbohydrates: 59 gm., Fat: 9 gm.

Croque Madame

Yield: 6 servings

Delicious, egg-free French toast topped with a cheezy mushroom sauce. Serve with steamed asparagus spears and cherry tomatoes for a hot lunch or light supper entrée.

Have ready:

½ recipe Mushroom Fondue, p. 65

1 C low-fat, dairy-free (vegan) milk
2 T unbleached or whole wheat
    all-purpose flour
1 T nutritional yeast flakes
1 tsp. pure maple syrup (optional)
½ tsp. salt

6 slices whole grain bread
cayenne pepper or paprika

Prepare the Mushroom Fondue as directed, but keep it covered and warm in the saucepan, instead of transferring it to a fondue pot.

Blend together the milk, flour, nutritional yeast, maple syrup, and salt, or beat with a wire whisk until smooth. Pour the batter into a wide bowl. Dip the bread slices into the mixture, one at a time as needed, turning several times until fairly well saturated.

Brown both sides of each slice well in a lightly oiled or non-stick skillet or griddle over medium-high, turning once. Keep the cooked slices warm while the remainder cook by placing them on a lightly oiled or non-stick baking sheet in a 250°F oven.

Top each piece of French toast with ¼ cup of the hot Mushroom Fondue. Sprinkle a few grains of cayenne pepper or paprika over the top to garnish.

Per serving: Calories: 154, Protein: 6 gm., Carbohydrates: 23 gm., Fat: 4 gm.

Blintzes

Yield: 15 blintzes (5 servings)

Light, cheesy, and "eggy" blintzes without the eggs or cheese! Top with a dab of fruit sweetened jam or a spoonful of Tofu Sour Cream, pg. 90, and/or unsweetened applesauce for a truly authentic flavor.

2 C unbleached all-purpose flour
⅓ C nutritional yeast flakes
½ tsp. non-aluminum baking powder
pinch of turmeric
½ tsp. salt
2½ C water
1 T canola oil (optional)

1 lb. firm regular tofu (about 2 cups), drained and mashed well
½ C firm silken tofu, drained and crumbled
1-2 T sweetener of your choice
1 tsp. vanilla extract
2 T fresh lemon juice
1 tsp. salt
½ tsp. ground cinnamon

To make the blintz wrappers, place the dry ingredients in a large mixing bowl, and stir with a wire whisk to combine well. Make a well in the center of the dry ingredients, and pour in the water and oil, if using. Mix well with a whisk until the batter is smooth.

If you don't have a non-stick skillet or crêpe pan, lightly oil an 8"-9" skillet; place over medium-high heat. When the skillet is very hot (water dropped on it beads and dances across the surface) pour on the batter, using a scant ¼ cup for each wrapper, and immediately swirl it into a very thin circle, about 5-6 inches in diameter. Cook over medium-high until the top surface is dry and the edges begin to curl up, about 2 minutes. Carefully loosen and turn the wrapper over. Cook the second side very briefly, about 30-45 seconds. Stack on a plate while the remainder cook. Re-oil the pan as necessary.

Preheat the oven to 350°F.

To make the filling, mash together in a large bowl both kinds of tofu, sweetener, vanilla, lemon juice, salt, and cinnamon into a smooth, finely grained paste. Mix well. For each wrapper, spread

...continued on next page

about 2 slightly rounded tablespoonfuls of filling in a horizontal line about 1 inch from the edge nearest to you. Fold in the left and right sides about 1 inch. Then roll the wrapper, starting with the end the filling is on, into a neat packet.

Place the blintzes on a lightly oiled or non-stick baking sheet, and bake for 10 minutes. Serve immediately.

Per serving: Calories: 300, Protein: 16 gm., Carbohydrates: 45 gm., Fat: 5 gm.

Aunt Shayna's Potato Cakes

Yield: 8 cakes (serves 2-4)

Aunt Shayna was from the "old country," and was an exceptional cook. She had a special way of making everything taste "warm and cozy," as though she had added an extra pinch of love. Aunt Shayna made these yummy cakes with grated onion, eggs, and leftover mashed potatoes. Here we eliminate the eggs and use instant potato flakes so they are healthful and unbelievably easy to prepare.

1 C low-fat dairy-free (vegan) milk
½ C quick-cooking rolled oats
1 C instant potato flakes
2 medium carrots, scraped and shredded
1 stalk celery, finely minced
1 small onion, grated
3 T nutritional yeast flakes
½ tsp. salt
freshly ground black pepper, to taste

Put the milk in a medium saucepan, and bring to a boil. Remove from the heat and stir in the oats. Cover and let stand for 5 minutes. Stir in the remaining ingredients, mixing very well. The mixture will be stiff.

Form into eight small patties using moistened hands, and place them on a sheet of waxed paper.

Heat a non-stick or oiled skillet, and slowly brown the patties on both sides. Serve hot or warm.

Per cake: Calories: 142, Protein: 4 gm., Carbohydrates: 29 gm., Fat: 0 gm.

Nino's Manicotti

Yield: 14-16 manicotti

These very special manicotti are made with homemade crêpes instead of store-bought pasta tubes. They take a bit of extra time to prepare, but if your sauce and filling are made a day or so ahead, final assembly will actually be quite quick. If you prefer to use the dry manicotti noodles, boil them until al dente according to the package directions. Stuff and bake them as directed below, pouring a little Marinara Sauce, pg. 92, over the noodles before baking.

Have ready:

1 recipe Marinara Sauce, p. 92,
    or 6 C of your favorite fat-free
    tomato sauce

1 C unbleached all-purpose flour
1 C whole wheat pastry flour
½ tsp. salt
2 C low-fat, dairy-free (vegan) milk
¼ C water
2 tsp. canola oil (optional)

1 lb. firm regular tofu, drained and
    well mashed
⅔ C egg-free (vegan) mayonnaise
1½ T fresh parsley, minced,
    or 2 tsp. dried parsley flakes
2 tsp. dried basil leaves
2 tsp. onion granules
1 tsp. garlic granules
½ tsp. salt, or to taste

Prepare the manicotti crêpes as for Blintz wrappers in the *Blintzes* recipe, pg. 152, using the flours, salt, milk, water, and oil listed here, and set aside.

Preheat the oven to 350°F.

To make the filling, mix the next seven ingredients, and stuff and roll the manicotti as for *Blintzes*.

Spread a cup or so of Marinara Sauce over the bottom of a large, shallow casserole dish. Place the manicotti seam-side down in a single layer over the sauce, and loosely cover with foil. Bake for 25-40 minutes until the filling is heated through. Serve with hot Marinara Sauce on the side.

Per manicotti: Calories: 150, Protein: 5 gm., Carbohydrates: 20 gm., Fat: 4 gm.

Bread & Fontina Croquettes

Yield: 20-22 croquettes (5-6 servings)

Crispy on the outside, moist on the inside, these convenient bread and cheeze balls are delicious plain or served with Marinara Sauce, pg. 92.

¾ C water
¼ C nutritional yeast flakes
3 T quick-cooking rolled oats
2 T fresh lemon juice
2 T tahini
1 T arrowroot or cornstarch
1 T onion granules
2 tsp. salt
1 tsp. garlic granules
½ tsp. mustard powder

1 lb. firm regular tofu, drained and
    mashed well
1 small onion, minced
2 tsp. dried oregano leaves
1 tsp. dried basil leaves
1 clove garlic, minced
freshly ground black pepper,
    to taste

3 heaping C whole grain bread,
    cut in ½-inch cubes

Place the first ten ingredients in a blender, and process until the sauce is completely smooth. Set aside.

Preheat the oven to 350°F.

Combine the remaining ingredients, except the bread cubes, in a bowl with the reserved sauce, and mix well. Fold in the bread cubes, taking care not to crumble them. Using ¼ cup for each croquette, place in slightly rounded mounds on an oiled or non-stick baking sheet. Bake 40-45 minutes until lightly brown.

Per serving: Calories: 260, Protein: 15 gm., Carbohydrates: 30 gm., Fat: 9 gm.

Noodle Kugel

Yield: one 8" x 8" kugel (about 9 servings)

Hot noodle kugel (noodle pudding) was a staple in my family while I was growing up. It is a unique food—a main dish casserole that is slightly sweet but oftentimes served with savory foods accompanying it. Noodle kugel can also be served for dessert topped with canned or fresh fruit in season.

Traditionally, noodle kugel contains creamed cottage cheese or pot cheese (a dry curd cottage cheese), sour cream, eggs, butter, and wide egg noodles. This delicately sweetened rendition captures the traditional flavor without the heavy dairy products that are customarily used.

Have ready:

1 lb. wide, flat noodles, (If you are unable to find egg-free wide noodles, use 1 lb. fettuccine broken into 3-inch lengths)

1 lb. firm regular tofu, drained and finely crumbled or mashed
1½ C egg-free (vegan) mayonnaise
5 T pure maple syrup
1¼ tsp. salt
1 tsp. ground cinnamon*

½ C seedless raisins
½ C ground pecans (optional)

Preheat the oven to 350°F.

Cook the noodles al dente, drain, and place in a large bowl.

Place the next 5 ingredients in a separate bowl, and stir until thoroughly combined.

Stir the tofu mixture and raisins into the cooked noodles. Mix thoroughly. Pack into an oiled or non-stick 8" x 8" baking pan, distributing the mixture evenly. Sprinkle the ground pecans, if using, evenly over the top of the noodles, and bake for 25-30 minutes. Serve hot, warm, or cold.

Per serving: Calories: 239, Protein: 6 gm., Carbohydrates: 28 gm., Fat: 10 gm.

*For variety, add a pinch of ground allspice, coriander, cardamom, ginger or nutmeg along with the cinnamon. You can also add chopped dried apricots or prunes along with or instead of the raisins.

Noodles & Cottage Cheeze

Yield: 8 servings

A soothing and satisfying entrée. The special flavor comes from slow cooking the onions until they are very sweet. It may take a little extra time, but the flavor and simplicity of the recipe make it well worth the effort.

½ C water + 2 T balsamic vinegar,
    fresh lemon juice,
    or non-alcoholic wine
2 very large onions, chopped

1 lb. bow tie or spiral noodles

1 lb. firm regular tofu, mashed or
    finely crumbled
1 C egg-free (vegan) mayonnaise
1 tsp. salt
freshly ground black pepper,
    to taste

Heat the water and vinegar, lemon juice, or wine in a very large saucepan or Dutch oven. Add the onions, cover, and cook over medium-high for 15 minutes, stirring once or twice. Remove the lid and reduce the heat to medium. Cook, stirring occasionally, for 15-30 minutes or longer if time permits (up to an hour), until the onions are very sweet and caramelized. If the onions begin to stick or burn on the bottom of the pan, add a tablespoon or two of water or wine to help loosen them.

While the onions are cooking, boil the noodles until al dente; drain well and set aside. Keep warm.

Stir the drained noodles into the onions, and mix well. Stir in the remaining ingredients, adding salt and pepper to taste. Heat over medium-low until warmed through, stirring often and watching closely so the mixture does not stick to the bottom of the pan. Serve hot or warm.

Per serving: Calories: 215, Protein: 8 gm., Carbohydrates: 23 gm., Fat: 9 gm.

Grilled Cheeze Sandwiches

Yield: 8 sandwiches

This gorgeous, orange cheeze makes wonderful, quick, grilled sandwiches. Leftover cheeze can be stored in the refrigerator for several days and used to make sandwiches at a later time.

1⅓ C water
½ C pimiento pieces, drained
⅓ C quick-cooking rolled oats
⅓ C raw cashew pieces
¼ C nutritional yeast flakes
3 T fresh lemon juice
2 T arrowroot or cornstarch
1 T tahini
2 tsp. onion granules
1¼ tsp. salt
1 clove garlic, chopped,
    or ¼ tsp. garlic granules
¼ tsp. ground dill seed
¼ tsp. mustard powder
¼ tsp. paprika
pinch of cayenne pepper

16 slices whole grain bread

2 fresh, ripe tomatoes, sliced
    (optional)

Place all the ingredients except the bread and tomatoes in a blender, and process until the mixture is completely smooth. Pour into a saucepan and bring to a boil, stirring constantly. Reduce the heat to low, and continue to cook, stirring constantly until very thick and smooth.

Spread the cheeze on your favorite whole grain bread, top with a tomato slice, if desired, cover with a second slice of bread, and place on a tray under the broiler for 1-2 minutes on each side until lightly browned, watching closely so the bread does not burn. If desired, spread the top slice of bread with brown or yellow mustard after broiling.

To serve as open-faced sandwiches, first toast the bread slices, then cover with the hot cheeze spread. Finally, top each serving with thinly sliced red onion and sprigs of fresh parsley or watercress.

Per serving: Calories: 224, Protein: 9 gm., Carbohydrates: 33 gm., Fat: 7 gm.

── Reubens ──

Yield: 8 sandwich halves

The all-time deli favorite—a hefty, Dagwood-style sandwich. Serve with the requisite dill pickle spears and perhaps a dab or two of stone ground brown mustard.

Have ready:

1 recipe Marinated Seitan from
    Cauliflower Benedict, p. 138
8 thin slices Swizz Cheeze, p. 21,
    Mostarella Cheeze, p. 22, or
    Colby Cheeze, p. 20

½ C egg-free (vegan) mayonnaise
3 T ketchup
2 T pickle relish, drained
1 tsp. onion granules

8 large slices whole grain sour-
    dough bread, rye bread, or
    pumpernickel bread
2 C low-salt sauerkraut, well
    drained

Stir together the mayonnaise, ketchup, relish, and onion granules for the Russian dressing, and mix until well combined. Set aside.

To assemble the Reubens, drain the marinated seitan and firmly squeeze out the excess moisture. Arrange it evenly over 4 slices of the bread. Distribute the sauerkraut over the seitan, followed by the Russian dressing. Top with the cheeze slices and the remaining bread. Place on a tray under the broiler for 1-2 minutes on each side until lightly browned, turning over carefully with a spatula. Watch very closely so the bread doesn't burn. Slice the sandwiches in half and serve immediately.

Per serving: Calories: 250, Protein: 23 gm., Carbohydrates: 27 gm., Fat: 5 gm.

Greek Salad

Yield: 5 servings

Makes a light, refreshing, warm weather meal. Serve it on lettuce leaves with pita bread and steamed rice on the side.

Have ready:

1 recipe Betta Feta with marinade, p. 28

2 fresh, ripe tomatoes, coarsely chopped
2 C cucumbers, thinly sliced (unwaxed or peeled)
½ C red onions, chopped
½ C whole Greek or pitted black olives

Place the chilled Betta Feta and its marinade into a bowl with the tomatoes, cucumbers, onions, and olives. Toss carefully. Serve immediately or cover and chill, stirring occasionally to make sure everything is evenly coated with the marinade. Bring to room temperature before serving. Store in the refrigerator.

Per serving: Calories: 175, Protein: 10 gm., Carbohydrates: 12 gm., Fat: 8 gm.

Caesar Salad

Yield: 8 servings

All the flavor of the world-famous delicacy—minus the raw eggs and dairy products!

1 C low-fat, non-dairy (vegan) milk
¼ C fresh lemon juice
6 T brown rice vinegar
2 T tahini
4-5 cloves garlic, pressed
½ tsp. mustard powder
2 large heads romaine lettuce, torn
    into bite-size pieces
½ C Parmazano, p. 25
freshly ground black pepper,
    to taste
1 recipe Croutons (recipe follows)

To make the dressing, place the first six ingredients in a blender, and process until completely smooth. Set aside.

Place the romaine lettuce in a very large salad bowl. Pour the dressing over top. Toss well to coat the lettuce evenly. Sprinkle in the Parmazano and pepper, and toss again. Add the croutons and toss gently but thoroughly one more time. Serve immediately; do not let the salad sit or the croutons will become soggy.

Per serving: Calories: 227, Protein: 10 gm., Carbohydrates: 33 gm., Fat: 5 gm.

Croutons

Yield: about 8 cups

Crispy and delicious. These croutons will not reach their full crunchiness until they have cooled completely.

8 C whole grain bread cubes

Place the cubes in a flat or shallow baking pan, in a single layer. Bake in a preheated 350°F oven, stirring occasionally, until toasted (about 30-45 minutes, depending on the size and type of pan you use). In warm weather, if you prefer not to light the oven, you can toast the croutons in a large, heavy skillet over medium-high heat, stirring often, until they are dry and crisp.

Per ½ cup serving: Calories: 35, Protein: 2 gm., Carbohydrates: 6 gm., Fat: 0 gm.

Chef's Salad with Pine Nut Vinaigrette

Yield: 10 servings

A robust salad that's sure to satisfy even the biggest appetite. Pasta, salad vegetables, cheeze, and croutons mingle together in a tantalizing pine nut dressing.

Have ready:

½ C Parmazano, p. 25

1 recipe Colby Cheeze, p. 20,
   Swizz Cheeze, p. 21, or
   Muenster Cheeze, p. 23
   (or a combination), diced

3 C Croutons, p. 161

¼ C pine nuts
1 C water
⅓ C fresh lemon juice
6 T umeboshi plum vinegar
4 T mirin
1 tsp. dried oregano leaves
1 clove garlic, chopped
⅛ tsp. freshly ground black
   pepper
1 lb. radiatore or corkscrew pasta,
   cooked al dente and drained
1 head romaine lettuce, torn into
   bite-size pieces
3 fresh, ripe tomatoes, seeded and
   chopped
1 small red onion, thinly sliced into
   rings

To make a pine nut vinaigrette, place the pine nuts on a cookie sheet or baking tray, and place in a 350°F oven or toaster over. Roast for 3-5 minutes, or until golden. Alternately, the nuts may be toasted in a dry skillet over medium heat, stirring constantly, for 3-5 minutes. Remove from the pan immediately, and place in a blender. (Do not leave on the pan as they will continue to roast and stick.) Add the next seven ingredients to the blender, and process several minutes until completely smooth. Set aside.

Place the cooked pasta and salad vegetables in a very large bowl. Pour the pine nut vinaigrette over everything, and toss. Sprinkle on the Parmazano, and toss again. Add the cubed cheeze(s) and croutons, and toss gently but thoroughly one more time. Serve immediately; do not let the salad sit or the croutons will become soggy.

Per serving: Calories: 190, Protein: 8 gm.,
Carbohydrates: 26 gm., Fat: 6 gm.

Sweets

Gazebo Cheezecake

Yield: one 10-inch cheezecake (about 16 servings)

This is a deli-style cheezecake—dense and hefty—with your choice of a graham cracker or caramel nut crust. Top with sliced strawberries, blueberries, or fresh peaches in season.

Have ready:

1 Graham Cracker Crust, p. 177, with ½ tsp. ground cinnamon added, or 1 Caramel Nut Crust, p. 178

1¼ C water
⅔ C pure maple syrup
½ C brown rice syrup
½ C raw cashew pieces
¼ C fresh lemon juice
4 T agar flakes
3 T arrowroot or cornstarch
1 T vanilla extract
1 tsp. salt

1 lb. firm regular tofu, drained and crumbled

Preheat the oven to 350°F.

Prepare the crust in a 10-inch springform pan. If using the Graham Cracker Crust, reserve ¼ cup of the crumb mixture for a topping.

Place all the ingredients, except the tofu, in a blender, and process until completely smooth.

Pour half of the mixture into a bowl, and set aside. Gradually add half of the tofu to the remaining mixture in the blender, and process until velvety smooth. Pour the mixture carefully and evenly over the prepared crust.

Return the reserved mixture to the blender, and gradually add the remaining tofu, once again processing until completely smooth. Pour over the mixture already in the crust, and smooth out the surface.

If using the Graham Cracker Crust, sprinkle the top with the reserved crumb mixture. Bake for 60 minutes. Cool at room temperature, then chill at least 4 hours before serving. The top may crack a bit while cooling; this is characteristic of cheesecakes. Remove the outer ring of the springform pan before slicing.

Per serving: Calories: 158, Protein: 3 gm., Carbohydrates: 23 gm., Fat: 6 gm.

Chocolate Almond Cheezecake

Yield: one 10-inch cheezecake (about 16 servings)

Have ready:

1 Graham Cracker Crust, p. 177,
   or 1 Chocolate Cookie Crust,
   p. 179

1½ C water
1½ C pure maple syrup
½ C raw cashew pieces
½ C unsweetened cocoa powder
4 T agar flakes
3 T arrowroot or cornstarch
2 tsp. almond extract
1 tsp. salt

1 lb. firm regular tofu, drained and
   crumbled

Preheat the oven to 350°F.

Prepare the crust in a 10-inch springform pan, reserving ¼ cup of the crumb mixture for a topping.

Place all the ingredients, except the tofu, in a blender, and process until completely smooth.

Pour half of the mixture into a bowl, and set aside. Gradually add half of the tofu to the remaining mixture in the blender, and process until velvety smooth. Pour the mixture carefully and evenly over the prepared crust.

Return the reserved mixture to the blender, and gradually add the remaining tofu, once again processing until completely smooth. Pour over the mixture already in the crust, and smooth out the surface.

Sprinkle the top with the reserved crumb mixture. Bake for 60 minutes. Cool at room temperature, then chill at least 4 hours before serving. The top may crack a bit while cooling; this is characteristic of cheesecakes. Remove the outer ring of the springform pan before slicing.

Per serving: Calories: 187, Protein: 4 gm., Carbohydrates: 28 gm., Fat: 6 gm.

Pumpkin Cheezecake

Yield: one 10-inch cheezecake (about 16 servings)

This creamy, spiced cheezecake is homey and inviting for special holiday gatherings or as a delightful surprise dessert any season of the year.

Have ready:

1 Graham Cracker Crust, p. 177,
   or 1 Caramel Nut Crust, p. 178

1⅓ C water
1⅓ C canned pumpkin
1 C pure maple syrup
4 T agar flakes
3 T arrowroot or cornstarch
2 T fresh lemon juice
2 tsp. vanilla extract
2 tsp. ground cinnamon
1 tsp. salt
1 tsp. ground ginger
¼ tsp. ground cloves

1 lb. firm regular tofu, drained and
   crumbled

Preheat the oven to 350°F.

Prepare the crust in a 10-inch springform pan. If using the Graham Cracker Crust, reserve ¼ cup of the crumb mixture for a topping.

Place all the ingredients, except the tofu, in a blender, and process until completely smooth.

Pour half of the mixture into a bowl, and set aside. Gradually add half of the tofu to the remaining mixture in the blender, and process until velvety smooth. Pour the mixture carefully and evenly over the prepared crust.

Return the reserved mixture to the blender, and gradually add the remaining tofu, once again processing until completely smooth. Pour over the mixture already in the crust, and smooth out the surface.

If using the Graham Cracker Crust, sprinkle the top with the reserved crumb mixture. Bake for 60 minutes. Cool at room temperature, then chill at least 4 hours before serving. The top may crack a bit while cooling; this is characteristic of cheesecakes. Remove the outer ring of the springform pan before slicing.

Per serving: Calories: 131, Protein: 3 gm., Carbohydrates: 21 gm., Fat: 4 gm.

Ricotta Cheezecake Pie

Yield: one 9- or 10-inch pie (serves 8)

Easy, no-bake cheeze pie always seems to conjure up warm memories, and never fails to attract a crowd.

Have ready:

1 Graham Cracker Crust, p. 177, or 1 Chocolate Cookie Crust, p. 179

1 C water
2½ T agar flakes

½ lb. firm, regular tofu, patted dry, and crumbled
1 (10.5 oz.) pkg. firm silken tofu, patted dry and crumbled
⅔ C pure maple syrup
3 T fresh lemon juice
2 tsp. vanilla extract
¼ tsp. salt

Prepare the crust in a 9- or 10-inch pie pan, reserving 1 tablespoon of the crust mix for a topping.

To make the filling, place the water and agar flakes in a small saucepan, and bring to a boil, stirring constantly. Reduce heat and simmer for 5 minutes, stirring often.

Meanwhile, blend the remaining ingredients for 1-2 minutes. Pour the agar mixture into the blended ingredients, and process for 2 more minutes, until velvety smooth.

Pour into the prepared crust. Sprinkle with the reserved crumb crust. Refrigerate until well chilled and set, about 6-8 hours or overnight.

If desired, top each serving with fresh whole raspberries, blueberries, or sliced strawberries.

Per serving: Calories: 217, Protein: 6 gm., Carbohydrates: 29 gm., Fat: 8 gm.

Chocolate Cheezecake Pie

Prepare as for *Ricotta Cheezecake Pie*, replacing the lemon juice with ⅓ C unsweetened cocoa powder, and decreasing the agar flakes to 2 tablespoons and the vanilla extract to 1½ tsp.

Peanut Butter Fudge Pie

Yield: one 10-inch pie (serves 10)

The dessert of choice for the chocolate lover in us all. Rich, fudgy, and peanut-buttery.

Have ready:

1 recipe Flaky Pie Crust, p. 176

1⅓ C water
3 T agar flakes

½ (10.5 oz.) pkg. firm silken tofu, drained and mashed
1¼ C pure maple syrup
½ C natural, unsweetened peanut butter
½ C unsweetened cocoa powder
2 tsp. vanilla extract
¼ tsp. salt

Preheat the oven to 400°F. Prepare the crust according to the directions given, but bake it for 20-25 minutes or until golden brown. Remove it from the oven, and cool.

To make the filling, place the water and agar in a small saucepan, and bring to a boil. Reduce the heat and simmer for 5 minutes, stirring often.

Pour into a blender along with the remaining ingredients, and process several minutes until completely smooth.

Pour the filling into the cooled pie shell. Refrigerate several hours or overnight before serving (best when served thoroughly chilled).

Per serving: Calories: 290, Protein: 7 gm., Carbohydrates: 39 gm., Fat: 12 gm.

Apricot Creme Pie

Yield: one 10-inch pie (serves 8)

A no-bake, chiffon-style pie that makes a glorious presentation.

Have ready:

1 recipe Flaky Pie Crust, p. 176

8 oz. dried apricot halves (preferably unsulphured)
1¾ C water

5 tsp. agar flakes

1½ (10.5 oz.) pkgs. firm silken tofu, drained and mashed
½ C pure maple syrup
1½ tsp. vanilla extract

9 apricot halves (reserved from above)
1 T brown rice syrup
1 T water
few drops of vanilla extract (optional)

Preheat the oven to 400°F. Prepare the crust according to the directions given, but bake it for 20-25 minutes or until golden brown. Remove it from the oven, and cool.

To make the filling, place the apricot halves and water in a medium saucepan, and bring to a boil. Boil for 1 minute. Remove from the heat and set aside until cooled to room temperature. Drain, but reserve the cooking water. Remove 9 of the most attractive apricot halves, and set aside for the topping.

Return the apricot cooking water to the pan, and stir in the agar flakes. Bring to a boil, reduce the heat, and simmer for 5 minutes, stirring often.

Pour into a blender along with the cooled apricots, tofu, maple syrup, and vanilla extract, and process several minutes until completely smooth. Pour into the cooled pie shell.

For the topping, glaze the reserved apricot halves by combining them in a small saucepan with the brown rice syrup, water, and vanilla extract. Cook until the liquid has evaporated and the apricots have a nice sheen. Place one apricot half in the center of the pie and the other eight evenly around the outer edge. Refrigerate for several hours or overnight before serving.

Per serving: Calories: 323, Protein: 9 gm., Carbohydrates: 48 gm., Fat: 10 gm.

Pineapple Creme Cheeze Pie

Yield: one 10-inch pie (serves 8)

Rich, refreshing, and irresistible. This pie is always a spectacular hit.

Have ready:

1 recipe Flaky Pie Crust, p. 176

2 (8 oz.) cans crushed, unsweetened
    pineapple, packed in juice
3 T agar flakes

1½ (10.5 oz.) pkgs. firm silken tofu,
    drained and mashed
½ C pure maple syrup
¼ C raw cashew pieces (optional)
1½ tsp. vanilla extract

fresh mint leaves, for garnish
    (optional)

Preheat the oven to 400°F. Prepare the crust according to the directions given, but bake it for 20-25 minutes or until golden brown. Remove it from the oven, and cool.

To make the filling, place one can of the pineapple in a small saucepan along with its juice.

Drain the other can of pineapple well, but reserve the juice. The easiest way to do this is to place a large, wire mesh strainer over a bowl, and pour the pineapple into the strainer. Press it firmly to remove as much liquid as possible. Set the drained pineapple aside.

Measure out ¼ cup of the reserved juice, and place it in the saucepan along with the other can of pineapple and its juice. Stir in the agar and bring it to a boil. Reduce the heat and simmer for 5 minutes, stirring often.

Pour it into a blender along with the tofu, maple syrup, cashew pieces, if using, and vanilla extract, and process until smooth. Transfer the mixture to a bowl, and stir in the drained, reserved pineapple.

Pour into the cooled pie shell. Refrigerate for several hours or overnight before serving (best when served thoroughly chilled). If desired, garnish with fresh mint leaves.

Per serving: Calories: 205, Protein: 4 gm., Carbohydrates: 31 gm., Fat: 7 gm.

Mocha Fudge Pie

Yield: one 10-inch pie (serves 8)

Decadently delicious! Fudge pies are typically made with chocolate squares containing hydrogenated fat, eggs, and high-fat dairy products such as butter and cream. This recipe proves, however, that sweet and rich desserts can be dairy-free and wholesome as well.

Have ready:

1 recipe Flaky Pie Crust, p. 176

¾ C water
3 T agar flakes
1 T instant, grain-based coffee
   substitute*

1½ (10.5 oz.) pkgs. firm silken tofu,
   drained and mashed

1 C pure maple syrup
¼ C raw cashew pieces (optional)
½ C unsweetened cocoa powder
2 tsp. vanilla extract
¼ tsp. salt
pinch of ground cinnamon

*Postum, Pero, Kaffree Roma, etc.

Preheat the oven to 400°F. Prepare the crust according to the directions given, but bake it for 20-25 minutes or until golden brown. Remove it from the oven and cool.

To make the filling, place the water, agar, and grain beverage granules in a small saucepan, and bring to a boil. Reduce the heat and simmer for 5 minutes, stirring often.

Pour into a blender along with the remaining ingredients, and process several minutes until completely smooth.

Pour into the cooled pie shell. Refrigerate several hours or overnight before serving (best when served thoroughly chilled). If desired, top each serving with a dollop of *Tofu Whipped Topping*, pg. 172.

Per serving: Calories: 248, Protein: 5 gm., Carbohydrates: 40 gm., Fat: 8 gm.

Tofu Whipped Topping

Yield: 1½ cups

A delicately sweetened dessert topping reminiscent of fresh whipped cream.

1 (10.5 oz.) pkg. firm silken tofu, drained
    and crumbled
2 T canola oil (optional)
2 T pure maple syrup
¾ tsp. vanilla extract
¼ tsp. salt

Process all the ingredients for several minutes in a blender or food processor until completely smooth. Chill thoroughly before serving and store in the refrigerator.

Per ¼ cup serving: Calories: 54, Protein: 3 gm., Carbohydrates: 5 gm., Fat: 1 gm

Chocolate Fondue

Yield: 3 cups (6 servings)

Serve with fresh strawberries, banana wheels, pineapple chunks, mandarin orange sections, apple wedges, and dairy-free (vegan) cake or cookies. Scrumptious and fat-free! This recipe is also a great hot fudge topping for dairy-free ice cream or a ravishing cold fudge dip or cake frosting.

2½ C water
¾ C pure maple syrup
½ C unsweetened cocoa powder
4 T cornstarch
1 tsp. vanilla extract
¼ tsp. salt

Place all the ingredients in a blender, and process several minutes until the sauce is completely smooth. Pour into a saucepan and bring to a boil, stirring constantly. Reduce the heat to low and cook, stirring constantly, until very thick and smooth. Transfer to a fondue pot, and keep warm over a very low flame.

Per serving: Calories: 150, Protein: 2 gm., Carbohydrates: 33 gm., Fat: 1 gm.

Easy Cheeze Danish

Yield: 4 servings

A light, quick breakfast, lunch, or dessert with the scrumptious taste of the venerated pastry.

4 slices whole grain bread

½ lb. firm regular tofu, drained and
    well mashed
¼ C pure maple syrup
1 T fresh lemon juice
1 T tahini (optional)
½ tsp. ground cinnamon
½ tsp. vanilla extract
¼ tsp. salt

Place the bread on a dry baking sheet, and set aside. Place the mashed tofu and remaining ingredients in a bowl, and mix thoroughly. Carefully spread the tofu mixture on the bread slices, covering the bread completely to the edge. Broil for several minutes until golden brown. Serve hot or warm.

Per serving: Calories: 168, Protein: 7 gm., Carbohydrates: 26 gm., Fat: 4 gm.

Mocha Java Junket

Yield: 6 servings

Sinfully luscious and creamy, this rich-tasting custard is sure to appease the most demanding sweet tooth.

1 C water
4 tsp. agar flakes
3 T instant, grain-based coffee
   substitute*

1½ (10.5 oz.) pkgs. firm silken tofu,
   drained and mashed
⅔ C pure maple syrup
1 T unsweetened cocoa powder
2 tsp. vanilla extract
¼ tsp. salt
pinch of ground cinnamon

*Postum, Pero, Kaffree Roma, etc.

Place the water, agar, and grain beverage granules in a small saucepan, and bring to a boil. Reduce the heat and simmer for 5 minutes, stirring often.

Pour into a blender along with the remaining ingredients, and process several minutes until completely smooth.

Pour into six small pudding bowls or custard cups. Refrigerate several hours or overnight before serving (best when served thoroughly chilled). If desired, top each serving with a dollop of *Tofu Whipped Topping*, pg. 172.

Per serving: Calories: 149, Protein: 4 gm., Carbohydrates: 29 gm., Fat: 2 gm.

Additional Cheezy Dessert Ideas

Chedda Topped Apple Pie

Prepare your favorite fresh or frozen apple pie. (Make sure the frozen one has no butter or lard in the crust.) Serve warm from the oven, and top each serving with a slice of *Colby Cheeze*, pg. 20.

Fruit and Cheeeze

Serve fresh fruit or berries with slices of *Muenster*, pg. 23, *Monterey Jack*, pg. 23, *Colby*, pg. 20, or *Swizz Cheeze*, pg. 21. Wedges of *Brie*, pg. 31, are especially elegant as a dessert cheeze.

Fruitwiches

For a snack or unusual dessert, cover crisp apple or pear wedges with *Gee Whiz Spread*, pg. 19. A tall glass of your favorite non-alcoholic wine or champagne makes this simple treat extra special.

Flaky Pie Crust

Yield: one 10-inch crust (serves 8)

Preparing flaky, whole grain pastry is not particularly difficult—the secret is in the technique. First of all the water must be ice cold, so if time permits, place it in the freezer about 15 minutes before using. The ice cold water helps the oil bind with the flour. Work quickly and handle the dough as little as possible to guarantee the flakiest results. This simple, delicious crust is ideal for any sweet or savory pie.

1 C rolled oats (regular or quick-cooking)

1 C unbleached all-purpose flour (or ½ C unbleached all-purpose flour and ½ C whole wheat pastry flour)
¼ tsp. baking soda
¼ tsp. non-aluminum baking powder
½ tsp. salt

¼ C canola or safflower oil
1 T fresh lemon juice
⅓ C ice water

Grind the rolled oats into a coarse meal in a food processor or blender. Place in a medium bowl along with the flour(s), baking soda, baking powder, and salt, and stir together.

In a separate bowl, stir together the oil, lemon juice, and ice water, beating briefly with a fork.

Pour over the flour mixture all at once, tossing lightly to moisten evenly. Form quickly into a ball, handling as little as possible. The dough might be slightly sticky, depending on the moisture content of your flour. Unbleached, all-purpose flour will make a slightly stickier dough; a mixture of unbleached, all-purpose flour and whole wheat pastry flour will be slightly drier.

Roll out the dough between 2 sheets of waxed paper to a circle slightly larger than the pie pan. (Moistening your counter before placing down the bottom sheet of waxed paper will help keep it from sliding.) Remove the top sheet of paper. Carefully flip the crust over, and lay it in the pie plate with the dough against the plate. Very carefully and gently remove the second sheet of waxed paper. Ease the crust into the pie plate without stretching or tearing it. Trim or turn under the edges and flute. Thoroughly prick the sides and bottom of the crust with the tines of a fork to keep air bubbles from forming under the surface.

To pre-bake the crust, place it in a preheated 400°F oven for 10-15 minutes. Remove it from the oven, and allow to cool before filling.

Per serving: Calories: 152, Protein: 3 gm., Carbohydrates: 18 gm., Fat: 7 gm.

Graham Cracker Crust

Yield: crust for one 10-inch springform pan (serves 16)

1½-2 C (depending on how thick you prefer your crust) finely crushed graham cracker crumbs (dairy- and lard-free)*

3-4 T granulated sweetener of your choice (optional)

2-3 T canola oil

Place the graham cracker crumbs in a bowl, and work in the oil and granulated sweetener, initially by stirring with a fork and then finishing the mixing by using your hands. Reserve ¼ cup of the crumb mixture for a topping, if you prefer. Lightly oil the sides of a 10-inch springform pan (or use one that has a non-stick coating—this works best), and pat the remaining crumb mixture evenly over the bottom.

Per serving: Calories: 49, Protein: 1 gm., Carbohydrates: 6 gm., Fat: 2 gm.

Cheezecake Pie Graham Cracker Crust

Yield: crust for one 9-inch or 10-inch pie.

Prepare as for the crust above, using 1-1½ C finely crushed graham cracker crumbs,* 2-3 T granulated sweetener of your choice (optional), and 2 T canola oil.

Reserve 1 tablespoon of the mixture for a topping, if desired. Pat the remaining crumb mixture onto the bottom and part-way up the sides of a 9-inch or 10-inch glass pie plate.

Per serving: Calories: 90 , Protein: 1 gm., Carbohydrates: 11 gm., Fat: 4 gm.

*Crumbs can be made by placing the graham crackers between sheets of waxed paper and crushing them with a rolling pin, or whirling the crackers in a food processor or blender until they are finely ground.

Caramel Nut Crust

Yield: crust for one 10-inch springform pan (serves 10)

1½ C pecans, finely ground
⅓ C quick-cooking rolled oats
1 T arrowroot or cornstarch
½ tsp. ground cinnamon

4 T pure maple syrup
2 T brown rice syrup, barley malt syrup, or dark corn syrup
1 tsp. vanilla extract

Place the ground pecans in a bowl, and stir in the oats, arrowroot or cornstarch, and cinnamon, mixing well. Add the remaining crust ingredients, stirring until thoroughly mixed. Lightly oil the sides and bottom of a 10-inch springform pan (or use one that has a non-stick coating—this works best), and carefully pat the crust mixture evenly over the bottom using lightly dampened fingers.

Per serving: Calories: 151, Protein: 2 gm., Carbohydrates: 13 gm., Fat: 10 gm.

Chocolate Cookie Crust

Yield: one crust 10-inch springform pan (serves 16)

1½-2 C chocolate cookie crumbs
  (dairy- and lard-free)*
2 T canola oil

Place the cookie crumbs in a bowl, and work in the oil, initially by stirring with a fork and then finishing the mixing by using your hands.

Reserve ¼ cup of the mixture for a topping, if desired. Pat the remaining crumb mixture onto the bottom of a lightly oiled or non-stick 10-inch springform pan.

Per serving: Calories: 54, Protein: 1 gm., Carbohydrates: 6 gm., Fat: 4 gm.

Chocolate Cookie Crust for Cheezecake Pie

Yield: crust for a 9-inch or 10-inch pie.

Prepare as for the crust above, using 1½ C chocolate cookie crumbs (dairy- and lard-free)* and 2 T canola oil.

Reserve 1 tablespoon of the crumb mixture for a topping, if you desire. Pat the remaining crumb mixture evenly over the bottom and part-way up the sides of a 9- or 10-inch glass pie plate.

Per serving: Calories: 86, Protein: 1 gm., Carbohydrates: 8 gm., Fat: 5 gm.

*Crumbs can be made by placing the cookies between sheets of waxed paper and crushing them with a rolling pin, or whirling the cookies in a food processor or blender until they are finely ground.

Glossary of
Special Ingredients

AGAR: Also known as *agar-agar* and *kanten*, this odorless, tasteless sea vegetable is a natural thickener and an excellent substitute for gelatin, which is made from animal products. Agar is available in three forms: sticks, flakes, and powder. The flakes tend to provide the most consistent results. If flakes are not available, use one teaspoon of agar powder for each tablespoon of agar flakes. Store at room temperature.

ARROWROOT: Arrowroot is a natural thickening starch made from grinding the whole root of the arrowroot plant. It is much less refined than cornstarch, and thickens at lower temperatures than either flour or cornstarch. Replace cornstarch with arrowroot measure for measure in recipes. Arrowroot must first be mixed with a cool liquid or water before using. Store at room temperature in an airtight, moisture-proof container.

BARLEY MALT SYRUP: Barley malt is a dark amber syrup with a light molasses taste. It is made from malted barley—barley which has been sprouted and dried (called diastatic malt). It is then ground, heated with water, and cooked into a syrup. Barley malt syrup is an excellent substitute for sugar, honey, or molasses in recipes. Organic barley malt syrup is made from organically grown barley. It is light in color and delicate in flavor. Because barley malt syrup is very sticky, it helps to lightly oil your measuring spoon before using, so the syrup will slide off easily. Keep barley malt syrup in a glass container in a cool, dry place, or in the refrigerator during warm weather to prevent mold and discourage insects.

BROWN RICE SYRUP: This is a delicate, mild sweetener. It is made from sprouted sweet rice which has been dried, ground, and then heated with water and cooked into a syrup. Store brown rice syrup in a tightly sealed, glass container at room temperature or in the refrigerator in warm weather to prevent mold.

BROWN RICE VINEGAR: Brown rice vinegar is a light, amber-colored vinegar with a low acid level, made from brown rice. It is delicate in flavor and tartness. Store it in its original container or in a tightly sealed bottle or jar at room temperature.

CILANTRO: Cilantro leaves are the small, fragile, green leaves of the coriander plant, also known as Chinese parsley. Cilantro has a strong, pungent, and distinctive flavor. It is an essential ingredient in many authentic Latin American, Asian, and Indian dishes. Store fresh cilantro in the refrigerator, and use within 3 days. Store dried cilantro in an airtight container away from light and moisture.

GINGERROOT: Gingerroot is the pungent root of the tropical ginger plant. Fresh ginger, with its slightly hot flavor and nippy aroma, is a fundamental ingredient in Asian and Indian cuisine. The peeled root may be minced, sliced, or grated before adding to recipes. Special porcelain and stainless steel ginger graters are available which make the task of grating much easier. For short-term storage, wrap fresh gingerroot in a dry paper towel, and store it in the refrigerator. For long-term storage, immerse peeled slices of gingerroot in canola oil, and store it in a covered container in the refrigerator. The flavored oil can then be used in cooking. You can also store fresh gingerroot in the freezer in a tightly sealed container where it will keep for up to 3 months. Just slice off the amount you need, and return the unused portion to the freezer.

LIQUID AMINOS: This non-fermented seasoning liquid has a deep, "beefy" flavor, similar to tamari. It is made from soybeans but contains no other additives or wheat. Tamari, shoyu, and liquid aminos are interchangeable in recipes. Although the recipes in this book specify only tamari, feel free to substitute liquid aminos measure for measure. Store liquid aminos in the original container or in a tightly sealed bottle or jar at room temperature.

MIRIN: Mirin is a mild seasoning liquid made from fermented sweet rice. It has a slightly sweet and distinctly Oriental flavor. After opening, store mirin at room temperature or in the refrigerator, tightly sealed in its original container. It may replace white wine or sherry in most recipes that require cooking.

MISO: Miso is a salty, flavorful, fermented paste made from beans and salt, and sometimes grains such as rice, barley, or wheat. It is used primarily as a seasoning. Miso ranges from dark and strongly flavored to light, smooth, and delicately flavored. Store miso in a tightly covered container in the refrigerator where it will keep for several months.

SEITAN: Also called "wheat meat," seitan (pronounced say-TAN) is cooked gluten, the concentrated protein in wheat. It is a versatile product that takes on the flavor of the seasonings it is cooked with. Chewy, hearty, and "meaty," seitan can be used instead of meat in many traditional recipes. It is available in jars, in the frozen foods section of natural food stores, or as a dry powder mix from mail order sources.

SORGHUM SYRUP: Sorghum molasses is a thick, sweet, dark brown syrup made from the cane-like stalks of the leafy sorghum plant (also known as sorgo). It is high in iron and an excellent replacement for honey, molasses, or other liquid sweeteners. Sorghum syrup occasionally has a tendency to crystallize, like honey. If this happens, place the sealed jar in a pot of very hot, not boiling, water until the crystals melt. Sorghum may be stored at room temperature in a tightly sealed jar, or in the refrigerator during warm weather to prevent mold and discourage insects.

TAHINI: Tahini is a smooth paste made from sesame seeds and is an essential ingredient in many Middle Eastern recipes. Tahini may be very thick, like peanut butter, or thin and slightly runny, depending on the brand. As with all unrefined nut and seed butters, store tahini in the refrigerator to keep it from becoming rancid.

TAMARI: Tamari is a naturally fermented soy sauce which is available in a number of varieties, including low-sodium, no-sodium, with wheat, and wheat-free. You may also find naturally fermented, wheat-free soy sauce under the name *shoyu*. Store tamari in a tightly sealed bottle at room temperature.

TEMPEH: Tempeh (pronounced TEM-pay) is a fermented, soybean-derived product made by inoculating whole soybeans with a culture. Tempeh has a pleasant, chewy, "meaty" texture, a nutty flavor, and an appealing aroma similar to cooked mushrooms. Tempeh is most commonly sold frozen in 8-ounce blocks and will keep in the freezer for about 3 months. Look for tempeh that is white with a few dark gray or black spots, the result of natural sporulation. Never eat tempeh raw. It should be cooked for at least 20 minutes and may be baked, broiled, steamed, or pan fried. After opening or defrosting, store tempeh in the refrigerator, and use it as soon as possible to avoid spoilage.

TOASTED SESAME OIL: This dark, aromatic oil, known for its tempting, delicious flavor, is made from toasted sesame seeds and used primarily as a seasoning. Store toasted sesame oil in a glass jar or its original container in the refrigerator.

TOFU: Tofu is a delicate, white cheese made by adding a curding agent (such as vinegar, lemon juice, calcium sulfate, or nigari) to soymilk, then pressing the curds into blocks and separating out the soy whey. There are two basic types of tofu: regular and silken. Regular tofu tends to be firmer than silken tofu and adds texture and chewiness to recipes. Depending on the manufacturer, regular tofu may come in one firmness only, or may be available in a range from extra firm, to firm, to soft. Silken tofu is actually made right inside its aseptic package. As long as the package is not opened, aseptically packaged silken tofu will keep for several months without refrigeration. Silken tofu also comes in a range including extra firm, firm, and soft. But silken tofu's overall consistency, unlike its "regular" counterpart, is very smooth and custardy, and therefore works best when blended with sauces and dips to add creaminess. Tofu should be stored submerged in water in a clean, covered container. Rinse the tofu and replace the old water with fresh water daily. Stored this way, tofu will keep for about 5 days in the refrigerator. Always rinse tofu and pat it dry before using.

TURMERIC: Turmeric is an orange-yellow spice used predominantly in traditional Indian cuisine. It is the dried and ground root of the turmeric plant, a member of the ginger family, and is an essential ingredient in curry powder, pickles, and prepared mustard. Turmeric's rich, festive color and pungent, slightly bitter taste make it adaptable as both a flavoring ingredient and coloring for food. As with other herbs and spices, store turmeric in an airtight, glass container at room temperature, away from light, heat, and moisture.

UMEBOSHI PLUM PASTE: Umeboshi plums are a variety of apricot which have been pickled in salt and an herb called red shiso leaves (beefsteak). They are used as a condiment in Japanese and macrobiotic cooking. The paste has a salty, tart flavor and makes a delightful seasoning. When using umeboshi plum paste, avoid adding salt to your recipe. Store it in a sealed container in the refrigerator, where it will keep for several months.

VEGAN MILK: Vegan milk is a generic term which refers to any creamy beverage such as soymilk, nut milk, or rice milk that is produced from non-animal products. Whenever vegan milk is called for, use the non-dairy milk that you most prefer or that fits in best with your dietary requirements. Store vegan milk in a tightly sealed container in the refrigerator where it will keep for about a week.

YEAST, HICKORY-SMOKED NUTRITIONAL: This light tan, dairy-free torula yeast has been hickory-smoked to provide a flavor similar to cured meats. Store it in a tightly sealed container at room temperature.

YEAST, NUTRITIONAL: Nutritional yeast, *saccharomyces cerevisiae*, is a natural whole plant grown as a food crop. It is prized for its delicious, cheesy taste and high nutritional content. *Saccharomyces cerevisiae* is a reliable source of high quality, easily assimilated protein and is the foremost natural source of B-complex vitamins; Red Star Nutritional Yeast T6635[+] is also an excellent source of vitamin B12. *Saccharomyces cerevisiae* is easy to recognize because of its yellow color which ranges from light tan to bright gold. It is an inactive yeast which means it has no fermenting power as does the live yeast used in leavening or brewing, rendering it more digestible. Nutritional yeast is not dried torula (*Candida utilis*), a yeast-like organism which is grown on waste products from the wood pulp industry, nor is it brewer's yeast or baking yeast. None of these products should ever be substituted in recipes calling for nutritional yeast.

Nutritional yeast is available in flake or powdered form. The recipes in this book call for flakes only, but if flaked nutritional yeast is not available in your area, use half as much of the powdered form. Some brands of packaged nutritional yeast have been combined with whey, a by-product of cheese processing. Pure nutritional yeast does not contain whey or any other dairy products, so read the product labels carefully. When kept in a cool, dry place, the physical characteristics and nutritive values of nutritional yeast remain unchanged for long periods.

Do not substitute ANY other yeast in recipes which call for nutritional yeast flakes.

Mail Order Suppliers of Natural Foods

The ingredients for the recipes in this book are generally available at well-stocked natural food stores. If you are unable to purchase locally the ingredients that you need, the following mail order sources should be of great assistance.

Ariël Vineyards
Napa, CA 94558
800-456-9472
An impressive selection of award-winning, premium wine which has been de-alcoholized through cold filtration. Contains less than ½ of 1% alcohol and has no added sugar.

Arrowhead Mills, Inc.
P.O. Box 2059
Hereford, TX 79045
800-858-4308
Organic whole grains, beans, seeds, flours, oils, peanut butter, and stupendous tahini.

Frankferd Farms
717 Saxonburg Boulevard
Saxonburg, PA 16056
412-898-2242
A certified organic farm, flour mill, and natural foods warehouse offering a wide selection of organic grains, flours, and macrobiotic foods. Family-owned and operated and committed to organic farming and food production.

Herb and Spice Collection
(a div. of Frontier Cooperative Herbs)
3021 78th Street
P.O. Box 299
Norway, IA 52318
800-786-1388
A dazzling array of non-irradiated herbs, spices, extracts, and flavorings along with related accessories. A good source for herbal seasonings, all-natural vegan bacon bits, and vegetable oils. Many products are available in bulk.

Gold Mine Natural Food Company
1947 30th Street
San Diego, CA 92102-1105
800-475-3663
A wide variety of macrobiotic items including misos, oils, nuts, seeds, beans, and non-caffeinated grain beverages.

The Mail Order Catalog
Box 180
Summertown, TN 38483
800-695-2241
Nutritional yeast flakes, tempeh starter, instant gluten flour for seitan, and TVP. Also many good books on vegetarian cooking and nutrition.

The Mountain Ark Trader
120 South East Avenue
Fayetteville, AR 72702
800-643-8909
Macrobiotic items and equipment. Also agar flakes, umeboshi plum paste, toasted sesame oil, and miso.

Vermont Country Maple, Inc.
P.O. Box 53
Jericho Center, VT 05465
802-864-7519
Pure maple syrup and granulated Maple Sprinkles.

Walnut Acres
Penns Creek, PA 17862
800-433-3998
Organic produce, fruits, flours, and grain, and one of the finest peanut butters available. Also a reliable source for hickory smoked nutritional yeast (Bakon yeast).

Index

Ask your store to carry our fine line of cookbooks or you may order directly from:

Book Publishing Company

American Harvest.....$11.95

Burgers 'n Fries 'n Cinnamon Buns.....$6.95

Cookin' Healthy with One Foot Out the Door.....$8.95

Cooking with Gluten and Seitan.....$7.95

Ecological Cooking.....$10.95

From A Traditional Greek Kitchen.....$9.95

George Bernard Shaw Vegetarian Cookbook.....$8.95

Instead of Chicken, Instead of Turkey.....$9.95

Judy Brown's Guide to Natural Foods Cooking.....$10.95

Kids Can Cook.....$9.95

Murrieta Hot Springs Vegetarian Cookbook.....$9.95

New Farm Vegetarian Cookbook.....$8.95

Now and Zen Epicure....$17.95

The Peaceful Cook.....$8.95

The Shiitake Way.....$7.95

The Shoshoni Cookbook: Vegetarian Recipes from the Shoshoni Yoga Spa.....$12.95

Soups for All Seasons.....$9.95

The Sprout Garden.....$8.95

Starting Over: Learning to Cook with Natural Foods.....$10.95

Tempeh Cookbook.....$10.95

Ten Talents.....$18.95

Tofu Cookery, revised.....$14.95

Tofu Quick & Easy.....$7.95

TVP Cookbook $6.95

The Uncheese Cookbook.....$11.95

Uprisings: The Whole Grain Bakers' Book....$13.95

Vegetarian Cookbook for People with Diabetes.....$10.95

To order, please include *$2 per book* for postage and handling.

Mail your order to: **Book Publishing Company**
P.O. Box 99
Summertown, TN 38483

Or call: **1-800-695-2241**